NADINE AND VINSON

NADINE AND VINSON

A TIME TO WEEP AND A TIME TO LAUGH

BY

Patricia Erwin Call

Mountain State Press
Charleston, West Virginia

International Standard Book Number: 0-941092-30-5

Library of Congress Catalog Card Number: 95-79653

First Edition

Mountain State Press
c/o The University of Charleston
2300 MacCorkle Avenue, SE
Charleston, WV 25304

Printed in the United States of America

Cover Design: Sharon Harms
                  Image Associates

This is a Mountain State Press book produced in affiliation
with The University of Charleston. Mountain State Press is
solely responsible for editorial decisions.

The source of *Nadine and Vinson* is love: The love shared between the people written about in this book; the love they showered upon me; and the love of my many friends who encouraged me to write this reminiscence. It is written to rekindle the warmth of two wonderful people for those who had the privilege of knowing them, for those who did not and especially for Nadine and Vinson's grandchildren, Mark, Rochelle and Patrick. I am particularly grateful to my husband, Doug, who has been uncommonly dedicated in helping me with *Nadine and Vinson*.

TO EVERYTHING THERE IS A SEASON . . .
A TIME TO BE BORN, AND
 A TIME TO DIE;
  A TIME TO PLANT, AND
   A TIME TO PLUCK UP THAT WHICH IS
      PLANTED;
     A TIME TO WEEP AND A TIME TO LAUGH . . .
                    ECC. 3:1- 4

The house that Vinson built
825 Saunders, street
Saint Albans, West Virginia

A
TIME
TO BE
BORN

THE BEGINNING

Nadine Ruth Miller was three years old in 1912 when she and her Aunt Vonzine boarded a train in St. Albans bound for Charleston. Nadine was given the window seat in hopes the passing scenes would occupy her during their fourteen-mile trip. Most three-year-olds would be excited about their first train ride, but Nadine sat quietly staring out the window at the layers of gray clouds which would not allow the sun's rays to penetrate. She watched rivulets of rain creep down the window pane, giving the appearance of tear drops.

"Vonzine, do you care if I sit beside you? The train is crowded this morning," a voice inquired.

Vonzine wanted to say, "Yes I care. I want to be alone." But a quick glance across the train compartment confirmed Liz Allen Goff Taylor's complaint. All of the seats were taken except the one beside her, and Vonzine had only paid fare for one adult and one child. Trying to force a smile, she scooted closer to Nadine, saying, "Of course, Mrs. Taylor."

Nadine heard the rustle of a long dress as Mrs. Taylor sat down, but the child did not look away from the window. There was a surge of steam, the sound of a whistle, and, with a jerk, the train was in motion.

"Seems I got seated just in time," said Liz. Receiving no response from Vonzine, she concentrated her attention on the little girl whose thick, shining, auburn hair flowed down her back, falling gently into curls. She held a soft fur muff with one hand inside and the other folded on top. Liz noted how small and delicate the hand was, even for a child her age. "Is this Phil and Hazel's little girl?"

Vonzine could not conceal her tension, for her voice cracked when she answered, "Yes." Knowing there were no secrets in a village the size of St. Albans, she leaned closer to Liz and lowered her voice, so the child would not hear.

Elizabeth Allen Goff (Liz) Taylor
Circa 1900

"I'm taking her to the Davis Child Shelter. Nobody in the family wants her."

Vonzine's voice, filled with emotion, raised with the last sentence. Nadine, wincing at these words, automatically pulled the muff closer to her small body and continued to watch Liz and Vonzine's reflections in the train window.

"After my sister Hazel died in birthing Nadine, Phil, who never could shoulder responsibility, took off, leaving the two children for Mom to care for. When Mom died six months ago, I took Nadine, and Phil's brother John, down in Winfield, took little Carl." Vonzine paused to gain control as her voice broke. But no tears came. Maybe the source of tears had dried up.

Nadine's hand shot forward, softly touching Vonzine's arm. At this moment, for the first time, Liz looked into the tiny freckled face with the green eyes flecked with gold, and the child openly looked back into the smiling blue eyes of this lady who was older than her aunt but younger than her grandmother.

"You certainly are a pretty little girl," said the lady. "Got red hair like your father." At this Nadine shyly shifted her eyes back to the window without turning her head.

Vonzine, having regained control of herself, went on, "As you might have heard, my husband has TB. The doctor says that if I insist on caring for him myself, Nadine cannot remain with me." Saying this she abruptly stopped talking, embarrassed that she had been so open.

Liz wanted to say, "I'll take Nadine; I'll take her." But not given to impulsiveness, she sat quietly, thinking. Being left a widow by Mr. Goff, she had married Mr. Taylor. He was now in his sixties and had never been healthy since fighting as a mere boy of fourteen in the Civil War. Neither had brought children to this marriage of convenience, only two large farms. Her farm encompassed Goff Mountain close to what is now Institute, and his was at Poca. Her heart yearned for a child. Oh, what a beautiful child this was, and she did know the

5

Dunlap and Miller families from which this child had been produced—good people fallen upon hard times. After all, this child's uncle, Dan Miller, had been a physician, and both he and Nadine's grandfather had been mayors of St. Albans.

She felt excitement build inside as her decision came into focus. Her temples beat, and the blood rushed to her face as she cleared her throat to say, "If you could only keep Nadine a day or two more, I'll ask Mr. Taylor if I may have her."

Vonzine's eyes searched Mrs. Taylor's face in disbelief. Here was God's answer to her prayers—not family taking Nadine, but yet not a stranger. A family of some means who would be kind. Vonzine, without hesitation, agreed

This was how my mother came to be reared by the Taylors. Sometime in the rearing, she became a free spirit. Was it not Nadine who, becoming bored with school, gave the passing postman a note to take to her Poppy Taylor saying she needed to come home due to her illness? This afforded her an opportunity to go home early, riding astride Poppy's gray horse Traveler.

Wasn't it Nadine who held a wake for a dead chicken and convinced her friend that indeed the chicken was levitating? Wasn't it Nadine who as a young woman gave the proper ladies of St. Albans the shock of their lives by sleigh riding down Main Street in the middle of the business day? Yes, she would never deny these things, and these incidents foreshadowed what would come later. The happenings I would hear, see and, indeed, be a part of as Nadine's only daughter.

Even though Nadine at age fifteen had the security of the Taylors harshly jerked away by their deaths, she never lost her free spirit. She fended for herself by clerking in stores and boarding with relatives, and the focal point of her spiritual growth and social life was the church. Here she attracted many suitors, but she was selective. As she would one day tell me, "Since the man you pick as your husband you also pick as the father of your children, you can't be too careful."

When at thirty Mother was not married, her friends were concerned. Preacher Myers, minister of the church, made the joke that he had seen Nadine down on her knees looking in a manhole for a man.

Then one day Vinson Erwin, my dad, "came a-courting." Instead of flowers, this slender young man, with soft brown eyes and high cheek bones, brought two quarts of big, red, delicious strawberries. Oddly enough it was this practicality that some say won Mother's attention.

Vinson's practicality resulted from his upbringing. He was raised in a seven-room white frame farm house built around the turn of the century. As a child, bedtime found him, his brother Earl, and three sisters—Ochel, Iola, and Ima—seated in the sitting room with the yellow firelight slanting across their five bowed blondish-red heads.

Their Poppy, using the light given off by the coal fire, so as not to waste oil in the oil lamps, would be having family devotions, as Mommy, after a hard day's work, half listening, nodded sleepily over the *Putnam Democrat Newspaper*. In this family, discipline was strict and the one-room school was attended only when there were no chores to be done. Though the Erwins were not directly affected by the depression of the 30s, its somber mood became a part of their personalities, leaving them frugal, industrious, and cautious.

At age thirty-one, this perhaps unlikely couple, Nadine and Vinson, were married on January 10, 1940. I was the first born, then David. Dad worked his entire married life at the local DuPont plant, and he and Mother changed addresses only once. Sound boring? Well, it was not. Mother had a way of keeping life at 825 Saunders Street busy and unpredictable. Nobody knew what might happen next. Or in Dad's words, "That woman has got me so bumfuzzled, I don't know which end is up."

The slow, dull, irregular scraping was barely audible above the busy street sounds of the 9:00 a.m. Charleston traffic in August of 1944. Step, scrape, step, scrape was the rhythm as my stiffened left leg pulled my foot along. Mother leaned over and picked me up, saying, "Hug Momma's neck. We're almost at Dr. Anderson's office."

Once on the doctor's examining table, I felt his firm touch as he bent first my right arm and then my right leg, but there was little yielding when he reached my left arm and even less in my left leg. The examination continued in silence as Mother stood on the opposite side of the table watching.

"Polio, Mrs. Erwin, your daughter has polio!" Dr. Anderson went on to explain, "Polio is a virus that attacks the central nervous system. It has, in Patty's case, caused some paralysis. Her muscles on the left side are drawing."

Mother pulled her clasped hands to her breast and stared out the window. Her eyes appeared to focus upon nothing.

"Mrs. Erwin," came Dr. Anderson's voice again, and again it aroused no response.

The doctor's comments were fixed on the present, but I later heard Mother relate to Dad that upon hearing the doctor's evaluation her thoughts flitted from the present to the past, to the present, and into the future. Mother said her prayer at that critical moment was, "My own mother died when I was three weeks old; only through your grace, dear God was I, at age three, spared from an orphanage. Polio—age three—my child, spare her, dear God from this crippling disease. Please, spare her . . . ."

"Mrs. Erwin?" the doctor's voice broke into her prayer.

"Yes, Dr. Anderson, I heard."

"The nurse will dress Patty. Come into my office. I need to call Morris Memorial Hospital in Milton to make arrangements for Patty's treatment. Is that all right with you?"

"Yes," Mother answered as she patted my arm and gave me a reassuring smile. "I'll be right back, Patty. Mind the nurse." She turned and followed the doctor as if she herself were an obedient child.

When I was older, through overheard conversations, I learned about the alternatives my parents considered for the payment of my treatment. They knew my treatments would take money—lots of money.

There was Dad's plant hospitalization. DuPont provided good coverage for its employees. Even this wouldn't be nearly enough money. There was the house that Dad had spent every free minute building for us. He cut the oak with which it was built from Grandpa's farm. He used a team of horses to drag the logs out of the woods along the mud roads which snaked their way beside Cow Creek and out to the main road that led to the lumber mill where the lumber was dressed out. The same team of horses was used to dig the foundation. Dad did the landscaping by hand with a shovel. Even with all this toil, there was money owed for materials which had to be bought at inflated wartime prices. Still, the house would bring some money. Whatever had to be done to provide my needed treatment would be done. Even if it took a lifetime to repay the debt, it would be done.

The same night, following my diagnosis of polio, I was driven to the hospital, twenty miles from St. Albans. There were four of us in our second-hand Hudson Terraplane: Dad, Mother, her brother Carl and me.

Mother and Uncle Carl did not see each other after their initial separation, when Carl was three and Mother was an infant, until Carl was fourteen. After this their visits were infrequent, but as adults they became fast friends. I would do things for Uncle Carl that I would not do willingly for other adults, like stop biting my nails or being afraid of thunder and lightning. Perhaps that was why he accompanied us, or perhaps my parents needed emotional support.

As our car moved along the dark road, its headlights catching the reflectors which marked curves, conversation was sparse. Mother's voice is all that I remember.

"Patty, there will be other children at the hospital and a big indoor swimming pool—like our bathtub only much bigger."

This explanation was necessary because at age three I had never seen a swimming pool. My pool was Cow Creek which flowed through Grandpa's farm. The silent salty tears seeped into the corners of my mouth.

"You're going to get all better and will run like before," Mother continued as she cuddled me close on her lap.

As the car turned off Route 60 onto a side road, its lights flashed onto a gray stone building with white pillars. After Dad parked the car, without a word, he placed me on his shoulders, horseback fashion, and carried me inside.

I cannot remember faces, only images of people wearing white uniforms, dimly lit corridors lined with wheelchairs, and silence. This would be my first night of separation from my parents. Many more followed.

In 1945, polio was more commonly called Infantile Paralysis because its incidence was higher among young children. The cause and spread were a mystery. It was thought that possibly the cause was flies, polluted water, or human carriers. The result of paralyzed and twisted limbs, even death, was a fact and made Infantile Paralysis a disease to be dreaded.

Health officers quarantined our house. My father did not go to work for a number of days. Even my dog Dutch had to be kept indoors. When Mother went shopping, after the quarantine was lifted, friends crossed to the other side of the street and yelled their inquiries and concerns. She certainly understood that no one wanted to be infected.

Mother, being a staunch believer in prayer, made prayer requests when asked what might be done. She later said friends, relatives, neighbors, and Dad's fellow workers who attended churches up creeks and hollows and in small and large communities earnestly prayed for my recovery.

Of course I was only aware of my own situation, not that of my parents. Following a period of isolation and observation, I was placed in the children's ward of the hospital. Through the eyes of a three-year-old, lying flat on my back in a crib, the area seemed huge. As I think back, I believe there had to be at least sixteen beds on both sides of the room.

I dreaded the time each day when the washing machines filled with steaming water were wheeled into the ward. Strips of wool blankets were pulled from the hot water, wrung out and wrapped around my afflicted limbs. Oh, how those wool strips itched! My mother called this the "Sister Kenny Treatment." The procedure relaxed my muscles for the physical therapy that followed.

I cannot recall visitors to this ward, but I do remember, after supper one evening, seeing a familiar figure in white approaching my bed. "Peek-a-boo," I heard, and quick as a wink I was staring up into Momma's smiling eyes. She had taken a job as a hospital maid to be with me. Due to her schedule, she went home only on the weekends. This meant Dad had to batch it five days a week.

Five evenings a week I could always count on Mother quietly tiptoeing to my bedside to read or sing to me and always to say my prayers, "Now I lay me down to sleep . . . ." Our favorite song was, "One little, two little, three little Indians . . . ." I had a surprise for her one evening, a jingle which contained the passage, "Catch a nigger by his toe. If he hollers, let him go . . . ."

As I proudly recited, the furrows in Mother's brow deepened. "Where did you hear that?" she quietly asked. I pointed three beds down to a little boy, the only black patient in our ward.

"He says that?" she questioned.

"No, they do. And then he laughs, too," I said.

"Who do you mean by they?"

11

I shrugged because I did not know, and "they" just wore white uniforms like everybody else.

"Let's not say it anymore," were Mother's instructions.

I did not understand Mother. Other people laughed at this, and she always liked funny things.

As I improved, Mother sometimes wheeled me down the corridors where I might look into a room and see a monstrous thing that Momma called an "iron lung." She said it breathed for the person that lay inside. To this day, I recall vividly the faint wheeze of those huge electrically powered bellows, moving in and out in a steady rhythm.

I was glad not to be in that iron monster. However, I would have enjoyed going to the elementary classrooms and to the auditorium where movies were shown or plays were performed by local school children, but I was either too young or too naughty. Once I thought I was going to a play performed by St. Albans High School students under the direction of Mr. Pittenger. However, on the evening of the performance, for disciplinary purposes, I was told I could not go. I can't recall my transgression, but I vividly remember watching tearfully as all the other children in my ward were wheeled away, leaving me alone.

I do have some pleasant memories of my hospital stay. In the evenings, Momma would hold me up to the window so that I could see the farm animals, especially the cows, grazing. I recall asking, "Why are the calves biting their mommas?" Mother explained that they were not biting but nursing. There was also the Olympic-size swimming pool where, when I was immersed, I could move my arms and legs almost as before.

After six months, I was able to come home, but my therapy continued. Each day Mother lifted me onto the dining room table to exercise my muscles as she had been trained to do. Thank goodness there were no more hot packs, just those hated, ugly, high-topped orthopedic shoes and the thick brown liquid iron tonic that was spooned into me daily to ward off anemia.

When Dad heard me complain, he reminded me that President Roosevelt had polio and wore a body brace. I heard respect in Dad's voice when he spoke of President Roosevelt.

We did not lose our house as feared, for in the same block where Mother and Dad rented while building our home lived Mr. Hopkins who held a position with the March of Dimes. It seemed this elderly man knew Mother as a clerk at Leonard's Hardware and as a Sunday school teacher at the First Baptist Church.

In the summer, while Mr. Hopkins sat reading the evening paper, he saw my dad, dragging in dirty and tired after working eight hours, driving an hour each way, and then forcing himself to work on our new house as long as there was "good light." Mr. Hopkins must have been impressed by this young couple because he assisted them in applying to the March of Dimes to obtain some relief from the high cost of my treatment.

As I gained strength, when the March of Dimes Drive was in full swing, I was invited by various charitable organizations to be a model for the good works the March of Dimes did. After a guest speaker explained the accomplishments of the March of Dimes, I moved between the rows of those attending to pass the container in which coins were dropped.

I was always proud to hear the jingle of coins as the container was passed with a picture of another polio victim who, just like me, had been helped by the March of Dimes to overcome this dreaded disease. I heard people whisper, "Isn't she a pretty little girl," motioning in my direction. Indeed, I did feel pretty in my new plaid taffeta dress with puffed sleeves, a white peter pan collar and a wide sash about my waist which Momma had made just for this occasion. Then, I would catch a glimpse of my ugly, brown, high-topped shoes.

My legs and arms were again straight and strong, and we still had a home. This story could end here, but such

13

traumatic events have an ongoing effect on the people involved.

I cannot list all the effects on our lives because I do not know them all. I do know that every time I sneezed, after having polio, Mother whisked me off to the doctor; this made bills. My dad, being very conscientious, hated debts. This created an ongoing struggle in our lives.

Mother, after passing through this time of darkness to what she viewed as light, seemed to take the struggle "tongue in cheek." Life was not a series of coincidences. A loving God answered prayers. Opposing this serious vein of theology, I am convinced, after years of observation, that Mother also banked on God having a sense of humor, and that even though He did not conveniently look the other way, He did forgive.

A

TIME

TO

PLANT

SUPER SALESLADY

Mother was demonstrating at a large department store in Charleston. Now don't get me wrong. By demonstrating, I don't mean she was carrying signs protesting social injustices. No, she was into one of her part-time jobs, demonstrating a product. This time it was cologne.

The Christmas season was upon us, and we needed extra cash. When the personnel manager of Sears phoned Mother to say several cartons of an off-brand cologne, in seasonal wrapping to appeal to the frantic Christmas shopper, needed to be sold before December 24, she had made the right contact.

Mother worked until nine each night, showing her wares. The first few evenings, Dad and I drove up to get her after work, knowing she would be tired.

Sitting in our parked car, I felt the excitement of Christmas building as I looked at the glittering red, green, blue, and yellow Christmas lights. Their glow magnified, yet softened, as I watched them through our frosted car windows. I could see and hear the small Salvation Army Band, dressed in their dark blue uniforms trimmed in red, concluding each Christmas hymn with a loud bang and clatter of their tambourines.

Shoppers darted from store to store buying Christmas treasures. It was the season of hope for the fulfillment of promises; and I knew, with Mother's working, my wish for the dimpled doll with lamb's-wool hair that could be combed and washed would come true.

My thoughts were interrupted by, "There's your mother," an announcement coming from Dad as he motioned toward Sears side door with the sign "Employees Only" hanging over it.

I recognized Mom's short rounded form and her familiar "Joseph's scarf of many colors" (made from scraps of yarn acquired at different rummage sales). The scarf was tied

17

tightly around her head as a shield against the cold wind. Only one lock of her bright red hair protruded. She stopped momentarily to drop change into the outstretched hand of a Salvation Army worker, then hastened on toward us.

The cold air that rushed into the car when Mother opened the door was quickly replaced by the warmth of her body against mine. I was busy tearing the wrapping off the peppermint stick which she brought me when I became conscious of a pungent sweet odor that now permeated the air. "Did you spill vanilla on yourself, Momma?" I asked.

Before she could answer, Dad said emphatically, "Nadine, you smell like a polecat!"

I was rolling down the window to breathe when his attention turned to me, "Roll that window up. You're letting cold air in and allowing that awful odor to escape. We'll be fined for polluting the environment. Phewww! What is that smell, Nadine?"

"That fragrance is a cologne which is supposed to smell like Chanel No. 5 but sells for half the price," answered Mother.

"It smells like Corral No. 5 to me," Dad replied. "Surely nobody bought any."

"I'll have you know husbands bought this cologne for their wives," Mother said with pride showing in her voice.

"Well, I hope they don't open their gifts before Christmas day, or you'll have some irate wives after you. It won't be because you are the other woman, flaunting the affection of their husbands, but a woman flaunting their husbands' good sense of scents and cents. How many unsuspecting husbands did you manage to take, Nadine?"

"I didn't take anybody. The cologne is packaged attractively and will make nice stocking stuffers."

What a sales pitch, I thought.

"How many stocking stuffers did you sell, Nadine?"

"I didn't keep count."

"Well, approximately? You are working on commission."

"Three," Mother reluctantly answered.

"Three cartons!" Dad asked in disbelief.

"No, Vinson, three bottles. But I'll do better from here on in." She sounded convincing.

"Not unless you marked it as a bug repellent or as an ingredient for an asafetida bag." These were Dad's last words on the subject as he piloted the car out of the parking lot into the stream of homeward bound traffic.

The next evening when we picked Mother up after work, my welcoming words were, "You sure smell good, Momma!" An alluring fragrance seemed to permeate every article of her clothing—even her Joseph's scarf of many colors.

"That certainly isn't the smell you had last night, Nadine. Why are you smiling like a Cheshire Cat? How much did you sell tonight?" Dad asked the questions without pausing for an answer.

"Three," Mother answered nonchalantly.

"Three bottles, and you've been up here all day," Dad said in a disgruntled tone.

"Three cartons," Mother answered triumphantly.

"You smell different, you haven't changed products, and you definitely have improved your sales. How?"

She paused to flutter her eyelashes a few times before giving an explanation.

Dad persisted, "Well?"

"Well, when the cosmetic lady is busy with a customer, I just walk over and spray myself with Chanel No. 5. Then when I show my product in its pretty package, saying it smells like an expensive cologne at only half the price, the customer just takes a whiff of me and buys my cologne. One man bought enough for a whole secretarial pool."

"The results of that could be too horrible to imagine," Dad said shaking his head. "Could be worse than the poisonous gas released by the Germans during the war."

Ignoring this statement, Mother continued in her own behalf. "I never tell the customer I'm wearing the fragrance that I'm selling."

"No, but that is what they are assuming, wouldn't you think, Nadine?" questioned Dad.

Mother's eyes widened as she raised her eyebrows, causing deep furrows in her forehead. She turned away to look out the window. This was her non-verbal way of saying, "I'm not up to pondering this deep moral issue at this time." or "We'll have to put that on the back burner until later."

KEEPING THE WOLF FROM THE DOOR

After-Christmas blues did not come to our house until four or five months following Christmas. Around this time, a notice might arrive in the mail containing the following message: *This is the final statement prior to turning your unpaid account over to our collection agency. At such time, if this account is not paid in full, your dentures will be repossessed.*

True, no one got false teeth for Christmas, but in February a dun for a doll carriage came. Mother knew Santa had brought the carriage, but Dad had overlooked this gift. The money in the budget for Dad's false teeth was paid to Woodrum's for the doll carriage. This was not brought to Dad's attention.

It all started innocently. Mother thought that with her part-time Christmas work the doll buggy was affordable. However, her money, after taxes, bus fare, lunch, etc., did not stretch as far as she had anticipated. Dad was not informed because he would have disapproved of her poor money management, and no one wants disapproval.

So, the game of borrowing from Peter to pay Paul was set in motion. To keep Dad's false teeth from being repossessed and from his knowing that such a threat ever existed, Mother was pressed into selling my record player. For two days, I hunted the house over for the missing record player. On the third day, there was my record player as good as new. In fact, it was new. Mother charged another record player identical to the first.

On the surface everything seemed to be quiet on the home front. Little did I know, and Dad knew even less. Mother, not being familiar with double entry bookkeeping necessary to keep track of all this wheeling and dealing, relied upon her own resources.

She was practically on a first name basis with the local loan company employees, pawn shop owners, auctioneers, and nurses at the blood donor center. Where, when worse came to worst, she would line up with the winos to sell a pint of blood.

The mailman posed a constant threat to her. By his placing the wrong piece of mail in Dad's hands, he could blow the whole operation. Mother kept our mailbox under constant surveillance, knowing exactly when the mailman should arrive. Tension always ran high at this time of day.

If Dad was working day or night shift, there was no problem. It was the four-to-twelve shift or his days off that took a toll on her nerves. It was on one of Dad's days off that either the mailman or Mom got off schedule. Mother heard the carrier stepping onto the porch. As she surged toward the front door, she looked out the window and spied Dad approaching the corner of the house.

She shifted into high gear, jerking the front door open. Not seeing a package in the mail which extended a bit across the storm door, she flung the door back with such force that it tore the mailbox right off the porch. The metal box fell to the floor, making a loud clatter and clang.

Dad rounded the corner just after Mom retrieved the box and pocketed the mail. "What was all the noise, Nadine?" he demanded.

Without hesitation, she replied, "I do declare, Vinson, the mailbox just dropped off the wall."

At about the same time the duns started arriving, the phone stopped ringing between the hours of 9:00 a.m. and 5:00 p.m., when Dad was at home.

I would hear him say, "Nadine, I haven't heard the phone ring today."

"Downright pleasant, isn't it?" she would answer.

"A silent phone is downright eerie to me," was Dad's reply.

It was during breakfast when he was voicing one of his pet complaints, "Nadine, I've told you over and over that a grapefruit half should be wrapped in wax paper, not a paper towel. The super absorbent towel has sucked the juice up. It's dry as a bone," when a knock came.

"Who could that be at this time of the day?" Mother questioned.

Dad yelled, "Come on in; the door is open."

Who should appear but the telephone repairman. "Mr. Erwin, I'm here to check your phone. You reported it out of order. It doesn't ring? Is that correct?"

"That's right. There it is. Go to it." Dad pointed to the phone and went on trying to mash juice out of his grapefruit.

Mother didn't move. She looked like one of those characters in a science-fiction movie who had been frozen in time.

The repairman took the bottom off the phone. I heard him mutter to himself, "What the . . . ?" as he looked at Dad, then Mother, and finally me with an expression which conveyed the message, "Is this for real?"

Reaching into the phone with his thumb and forefinger, he started to unravel what seemed to be an endless streamer of toilet paper which had been placed between the bells. "No wonder the phone doesn't ring, with the bells wrapped in toilet paper. Strangest thing I've ever seen. Has the phone ever rung since it was installed?"

Dad, glancing up briefly, pondered the situation and said, "If my memory serves me right, the phone has not been on the blink for the entire five years—just off and on."

We turned and looked at Mother for any input she might contribute. To gain time to think, Mother slowly took a drink of coffee, shifted her body in the chair, and carefully placed her fork on the edge of her plate.

She probably would have said the phone came that way from the factory, but that excuse had been eliminated. "You know it had totally slipped my mind, but one day while you were on midnights, Vinson, the phone kept ringing. So as not to wake you up, I just put that paper in to soften the ring. I guess it just stopped the ring altogether, and I plumb forgot about it." At that, she busily started clearing the dishes.

Dad directed the repairman to install phone jacks with a central bell system, so no such oversight could occur again. And by hook or crook, Mother got the bills paid by September—just in time for another Christmas.

WHO IS THE WEIRDO?

The Grand Opening of the new Sears and Roebuck store in Charleston, when I was a child, brought a great deal of excitement.   There were special sales, drawings for prizes, and the anticipation of having a wider selection of merchandise.

West Virginians, living in a state which was mostly rural, had developed a special familiarity, fondness, and loyalty to the Sears Company which revolved somewhat around the company's mail-order catalog.   The catalog allowed those living up hollows, in small towns, in mining camps, and on farms to keep abreast of the latest in fashions, furnishings, tools, and equipment.

Then, as today, the best time to relax and unwind was while on the toilet.   In the places and times to which I make reference, indoor plumbing was futuristic.   The outdoor toilets (johns) were in vogue, so to speak.

Nadine and Vinson, having lived on small farms prior to Vinson's getting his job at a local plant, had each spent many hours in the john pouring over the catalog or "wish book" as it was fondly called.   They, as others, found the catalog useful for more than entertainment and enlightenment-a functional use.

We won't discuss the functional aspect here.   I only wanted to establish the reasons for the popularity of Sears which culminated in a particular interest in the store's Grand Opening.

When Dad got home from work on the big day, supper was on the table so that we could eat and drive twelve miles to Charleston, arriving early enough to do some browsing.

Some time, while browsing at Sears, Momma strayed away from Dad and me, or vice versa.   We never settled who strayed first, even though the issue was aired on several occasions.   Anyway, after some time had passed, Dad checked his watch and said that the store would be closing soon, and we needed to leave.   We looked for Momma but couldn't find her.

"Every time we go any place, we end up getting strung out like a bunch of cows," Dad grumbled, as he directed me to the front exit.

"Aren't we going to wait on Momma?"

"We'll wait in the car."

Looking back, as we wandered through the parking lot searching for our car, I saw a guard closing the store door. I locked my knees and refused to move, screaming, "They're locking my Momma up! They're locking my Momma up!"

"I always expected it," Dad dryly responded. This made me scream louder.

"Calm down. I was just kidding. Can't you take a joke? Get in the car, and I will go get your mother."

Feeling Dad's firm lead, I unlocked my knees, and we went to the car. After being locked in the car, I watched Dad walk to the now empty store. Empty, that was, with the exception of the guard whom I could see and hopefully Momma whom I could not see.

Dad politely knocked on the glass door—no response. He knocked again more forcefully. This time the guard pointed to his watch and waved Dad away. Dad, not adept in sign language, seemed unable to get the message across to the guard that his wife was locked inside.

He would knock and point inside, and the guard would in turn shake his head and point outside. The gestures became more and more vehement and pronounced as the non-verbal exchange continued.

When Dad reached into his pants pocket to pull out his handkerchief, the guard jumped to his feet, poised for anything. Dad proceeded to fold the handkerchief into a triangle and tie it over his head in the fashion a woman might wear a scarf. He then pointed inside again.

At this, the guard unholstered his gun and unlocked the door. "I don't know what kind of weirdo you are, Mister,

although I have my opinion, but I told you the store is closed."
At that he slammed and locked the store door.

Dad turned and walked to the car. By the force with which he opened the door, I knew he was upset. I wanted to cry but knew better.

"I'll never know how that woman gets me in such predicaments. Did you hear that guard call me a weirdo? Wait until he encounters Nadine. Then he'll know what a weirdo is."

At this I began whining, "Where is my Momma?"

"She is probably up in the furniture department sitting on a sofa reading the funny papers while I almost get shot." He drummed his fingers on the dashboard and added, "She probably is reading about herself in the funny papers."

"No she isn't! There is Momma now!" I jumped up and down clapping my hands.

The guard unlocked the store door in a jovial manner. Mother strolled out across the parking lot, popping M & Ms into her mouth.

"Do you see that? There she is as relaxed as can be while I was called a weirdo and almost got shot. It's a wonder I'm not in jail now on attempted robbery charges."

I unlocked the door on my side to let her in.

"Where you been, Nadine?" demanded Dad.

"Here, I thought it was 7:30 and it's 9:20," said Momma. "My, time does fly. I was just browsing through the store. They do have the finest restrooms."

"Momma, I didn't know you were in the funny papers."

"Patricia, be quiet," Dad interrupted.

"Vinson, you sound disturbed."

"I've got a right. Here I am making a fool of myself running around with a handkerchief tied on top of my head, get accused of being a weirdo, and almost get shot while you're checking out the restrooms." He went on and on, while we listened and ate chocolate covered peanuts.

"I'm bored. There is nothing to do around here."

"Go play with Judy," Mother answered me as she stared out the window that overlooked Dad's vegetable garden.

"Judy went to her grandmother's. Her grandmother just bought a TV I wish we had a TV Everybody is getting one."

"We barely get our bills paid as it is. I don't think your father will put his stamp of approval on obligating us to one more monthly payment."

"Well, then, let's go to the movies," I suggested. "At least we would be nice and cool. It's so hot I can't stand it."

"I don't have the price of a movie," she said, seeming to be mesmerized by a bee darting right above Dad's tomato plants. "I used refunds from pop bottles to buy you that sky cone from the ice cream truck last night."

I let out a long wistful sigh, "Awwwwwwww," hoping to prod Mother into being her usual resourceful self. I knew that I had been successful when I saw that "try harder look" creeping across her face—the look that created those two wrinkles right between her eyebrows.

Shifting my body and placing my hands on my hips, I dropped my head in a sorrowful manner. Body language worked wonders with Mother.

It wasn't long before Mother bolted upright in her chair as if a current of electricity had passed through her. "Unless," she said, "you would want to go into the produce business."

"What do you mean?" I asked, fearing that I was on my way to being an accomplice in crime.

"Tomatoes," Mother said.

"Tomatoes," I echoed.

"We can sell your Dad's tomatoes. They'll bring a nice price."

I felt the pressure of my hand pressing against my throat as I gasped, "Oh, Mother."

"Don't be silly; we'll just sell enough to go to the movies. We can't possibly eat all those tomatoes," she said with a shrug.

So before I knew it, carrying a basket full of my dad's prized tomatoes, I had become a door-to-door produce peddler. Who could resist buying the perfectly shaped, flawless tomatoes from such a sad faced child? Nobody. My basket emptied quickly, and I hurried home to have Mother count my spoils.

"There is just enough for one bus fare downtown and back, plus an adult movie ticket, one child's movie ticket, and a bag of popcorn," Mother said after counting all of the pennies, nickels, and dimes.

"Oh no! How am I going to ride the bus if there is only fare for one?"

"That's a good point," Mother answered as she surveyed the room for anything that might be sold. But the pickings were scarce by this time of the summer. "Maybe we should go another day."

"Oh no! You promised!" I persisted with tears gathering in my eyes.

"Children under six ride free." She was talking out loud.

"But, I am nine going on ten and big for my age," I said indignantly.

"Well, we'll let that be our secret. Just slump down like this." Mother demonstrated. She rounded her shoulders, pulled her head down, and bent her knees just slightly. "See, you can reduce your height by at least one and a half inches."

"You look like a cross between the hunchback of Notre Dame and a turtle walking on his hind legs."

"Do you want to win the good posture award or go to the movies?" questioned Mother.

29

"Go to the movies," was my reply.

Mother then proceeded to hatch a plot.

"Go straight to the back of the bus as fast as you can. I'll be putting money in the meter. The bus driver will hardly know you are there. Don't say a word. Ladies don't reveal their true age anyway," Mother added as an afterthought.

"What happens when we get off the bus?"

"We'll use the backdoor, so we won't have to pass the bus driver again."

The bus trip went as planned. Thank goodness we didn't see anyone we knew. I would have died of embarrassment.

At the theater, Mother and I sat in the cool darkness, sharing a bag of popcorn. As we watched Judy Garland dance and sing herself across the screen, we escaped into a world of fantasy where pop bottles need not be refunded to buy an ice cream cone. However, reality struck on our way home.

"Give me the nickel for bus fare," said Mother, as the headlights of the bus could be seen coming in our direction.
"I don't have a nickel—only three pennies. There was tax on the popcorn."

"Oh, Lord," she pleaded.

I knew that if the bus had not been upon us, we would have been down on all fours groping in the darkness for two unclaimed pennies or checking the return lever on the pay telephone to see if someone had forgotten his nickel. But, too late, the bus was here.

"Do as you did before," Mother commanded.

So, I assumed my turtle stance once again. It was hard to walk very fast with my knees all bent, but this was no time to complain.

When I neared the back of the bus, I heard "clink, clink, clink" as the three pennies fell into the meter. The floor of the bus vibrated as Mother moved speedily in my direction.

"Lady, that's only three cents. Where are you going?" asked the bus driver in a not too friendly tone.

"Saunders Street," Mother replied as she kept moving.

"The fare for one adult is a nickel," said the bus driver as he turned in his seat looking at me suspiciously.

"Just take me as far as three cents will go," answered Mother.

My heart beat rapidly as I gripped the edge of the bus seat. I think I stopped breathing. We might end up in jail, I thought. Dad always said that Mother would get us all sent up the river someday. The bus driver turned back around in his seat shaking his head in disbelief. He put the bus in gear and maneuvered the vehicle in the direction of my home. Luckily there was only one other passenger, a wino.

He seemed to think everything was status quo as he sneaked a swig from his concealed wine bottle.

The bus stopped smack in front of Saunders Street.

"Bless you, sir," were Mother's departing words to the driver. He nodded.

I was just glad she kept his attention as I slowly exited the bus so as not to unfold like an accordion, revealing my true size.

The next morning I was awakened by the slam of the screen door and Dad's voice, "Somebody has been in my tomatoes." The only answer was the loud clanking and banging of pots and pans as Mother washed the dishes.

"Nadine, did you hear me?"

"What, Vinson?"

"I said," retorted Dad, "somebody has been in my tomatoes."

"Tomatoes?" echoed Mother.

"Yes, tomatoes. There are a bunch gone."

No response.

"Did you hear me, Nadine?"

31

"Um, hum," answered Mother as the clatter of pots and pans became louder.

"What could have happened to my tomatoes? They were there yesterday afternoon."

"Animals eat vegetables," stated Mother very factually. "Moles eat turnips."

"What kind of animal eats tomatoes?" inquired Dad.

"Rabbits," Mother offered.

"Rabbits don't eat tomatoes."

"Foxes eat grapes. Maybe it was a farsighted fox," Mother continued.

"I think you finally hit the nail on the head, Nadine. It was a red-headed fox that got my tomatoes."

Mother did not answer. She knew when to leave well enough alone.

MORE BUS RIDES

"Are we going to little town or big town, Momma?" was my question when as a child I dressed to go to St. Albans or Charleston. Little town referred to St. Albans, population 10,000, and big town meant Charleston, population 74,000. Big town was the answer hoped for because it offered more variety, and it took longer to get there by bus—our main mode of transportation. The longer ride provided more opportunity for exciting things to happen.

As we rode along, I entertained myself by matching up my fellow passengers. I tried to decide how people who boarded the bus together might be related or connected.

Since there were so few blacks, I decided they should be kin or at least know each other. If they didn't act friendly toward one another, I was puzzled.

There were other things to think about, such as the little boy who boarded the bus wearing a paper bag over his head. His mother held his hand tightly as she guided him to the empty seat in front of Mother and me.

I punched Momma in the side, pointed, and stifled a giggle. Furrows appeared in Mother's brow as she placed her index finger across her lips and shook her head. This familiar message meant, "Shut up and don't point." I complied and scooted back in the seat.

My imagination went into play. Maybe the boy had a dreaded contagious disease or the head of a monster. Maybe he, like my friend Cecilia, had lice and had to have his head shaved and painted with that ugly purple medicine.

Or perhaps, he had no head at all. This thought caused my mouth to fly open in a gasp. Mother gave me another one of those looks, but she too must have been caught up by curiosity. She tapped the little boy's mother on the shoulder and politely said, "My little girl and I are wondering why your

33

son has a bag over his head. Is he going to a masquerade party? Halloween is three months away, you know."

The little boy's body turned in the direction of Mother's voice. I could hear him breathing. This faceless body gave me the creeps, and I moved closer to Momma.

The mother's face flushed as she patted the headless form. "No, no, nothing like that. Joey was playing with my pots and pans and pulled a pot down on his head. Now I can't get it off."

A sobbing sound came from within the bag. "Momma almost screwed my head off, and then she pulled and pulled."

"Yes, yes, I tried everything. I even greased his head. Joey refused to come on the bus with a pot on his head, so I covered it with a bag," she said.

Mother sat upright in her seat. Challenge always invigorated her. "Did you try running hot water over his head to loosen the pan?"

Joey's mother shook her head slowly in the negative.

"How about tapping the pan with a blunt instrument. Did you try that?

The young mother's eyes widened and reflected a questioning attitude.

Mother, sensing that the lady was becoming a bit leery of her, quickly added, "I just wondered. When I can't get the metal rims off my canning jars, those two methods work."

The headless body's sobs could be heard again, but his mother's body relaxed after Mother explained her reasoning.

Following a few seconds of silence Mother asked, "Are you taking him to a blacksmith or a welder?"

I'll know never to put a pot on my head, I thought. *Mother would have it removed by a blow torch.*

The headless form's sobs intensified.

"No, no," the Mother answered. "We're going to the emergency room."

Mother's usual smile reversed with the corners of her mouth no longer curving upward but downward. That solution was too tame for her taste.

Not all of our bus rides were so entertaining. Sometimes we were the entertainment.

When I went to the doctor for my annual check up, Mother always insisted I wear a brand new set of underwear. This particular time my new underpants were too big. But, since we were running late, which was the norm for us, Mother did not have time to take a tuck in the waist. She told me to keep my stomach stuck out, and everything would be fine.

As the bus approached the stop where we were to get off, I felt Mother take my hand in hers, tensing up for a speedy departure from the bus and a fast-paced walk for the additional block to Dr. Basman's office. Mother was poised in a sprinting position. When the bus jolted to a stop, she jerked me up and pulled me along at such a pace that I can't recall my feet hitting the three steps that led off the bus. I just remember my feet suddenly hitting the sidewalk.

Mother, her eyes fixed on the red traffic light, never looked in my direction, assuming that since she had my hand that the rest of my body would follow her lead. The light flashed green, and she took off at a trot holding my hand in hers. However, when my arm had stretched as far as it could, she came to an abrupt halt. Her eyes still intent on the cross light, she said, "Patty, come on now, Dr. Basman is not going to give you a shot."

Her attention was only drawn from the traffic light by a series of loud raps on the bus windows and a man's voice, "Mam, I think your daughter has a problem." Seeing the amused looks on the passengers' faces, she looked down to see that my feet were encircled by my underpants, rendering me helpless.

"I forgot to keep my tummy pushed out," I said, as I continued my struggle, becoming more entangled.

Mother reached down, jerked my pants up, and quickly tied a knot in the elastic. We continued our race to the doctor's office as people turned and stared at the little girl with the peculiar knot protruding from her stomach.

Even when I was older, riding the bus was eventful. If we came up short on bus fare, as I mentioned earlier, I had to appear to be six years old, for those six or under rode free. Appearing six when I was nine required me to shrink in size by hunching my shoulders over, pulling my head down, and bending my knees. Then I would move to the back of the bus quickly while Mother deposited her fare. I did this so often that I became quite adept.

The last time I did it, I must have done such a good job that indeed I became invisible to the bus driver. When we arrived at our destination, in getting off the bus, Mother went first with me close at her heels.

The bus driver, seeing only Mother, closed the rear door as soon as he saw her safely dismount. This left all of my body outside of the bus with the exception of my left foot, on which the door had closed securing it inside the bus.

The driver put the bus in gear and started on his way. As I treaded air with my right foot, Mother was holding me securely against the side of the bus while running along beating on the bus with her fist and screaming.

The bus driver, hearing the commotion, looked around to see me in a spread eagle position, half in and half out of the bus. He slammed on the brakes and unlatched the door. He hesitated only long enough for me to complete my exit. Then, the driver proceeded down the road, nervously glancing back to see if I was all right and probably thinking that he would be sued—not because of my injuries—but because he had been responsible for stretching me, increasing my height two inches. No doubt he was amazed at the elasticity of my body.

LOST
SOMETIMES FOUND - SOMETIMES NOT

Hints from Heloise would not have been a frequently sought book at my home, if sought at all. My mother, being a people person, was not a house cleaning enthusiast. I often heard her say she wished we lived in a tent, so when it got dirty she could just relocate rather than clean.

Needless to say there was not a place for everything, nor was everything in its place. So, we spent a great deal of time and energy hunting for misplaced items.

Hunting for the lost telephone was most challenging. You see, we had telephone jacks which allowed the phone to be plugged in and used in different rooms. Unfortunately this meant that the phone could be unplugged, and anything not attached was a candidate for being a misplaced item.

The centrally located bell rang whether the phone was connected or not. When the ringing started, the hunt began. Anyone in the house at the time of the initial ring might participate in the hunt. This included friends and neighbors.

Often during the confusion of the search, Mother could be heard saying, "Someone has misplaced the telephone again."

"Yes," my father would agree in a not so agreeable tone, "someone certainly has!" giving my mother a knowing look.

The first ring started the hunt, the third ring served to move the searchers into a faster pace, and by the fifth ring the search had reached a frantic race.

Upon finding the phone tucked in the dirty clothes basket or any other such logical place, the hunt went into the second phase—plugging the phone into a jack before the final ring. Then, phase three would be to answer the phone, thus making contact with the outside world. If the answer could be accomplished with a reasonably calm voice, the caller could be deceived into thinking that he or she was communicating with someone in a "normal household."

Of course, the other participants in the hunt for the phone knew better. They sat on the sofa or possibly on the floor with pale complexions and wheezing sounds escaping their lips.

If the search ended unsuccessfully, by this I mean the phone was never located at all or it was found and not plugged in before the ringing stopped, the participants in the hunt would return to the activities that they were involved in prior to the search with bodies taut waiting for the next call.

Following one of the successful hunts, Mother, being the first to locate and connect the phone, answered in what father referred to as her "telephone voice." To her delight, she was being called to demonstrate Roly Poly Sausage at the local supermarket. This was a part-time job that afforded her some spending money of her very own.

Upon completing the arrangements on the phone, she immediately discharged me to the laundry room in the basement to iron her white uniform. To conform to Roly Poly Sausage Company's policy, Mother was to be clad in white from head to foot.

I carried out the assigned task without complaint because Mother's spending money was always freely shared with me. Intent on doing my ironing well, I only glanced over my shoulder when I heard a squeak at the top of the stairs. Seeing it was Mother coming down, I continued ironing.

I heard Dad's half-used paint cans being moved about. In a few minutes, I thought I caught a whiff of paint. Finished with my ironing, I switched the iron off and hung the uniform on a hanger. Turning to go back upstairs, I saw Mother bent over, seeming to be in a state of deep concentration—no doubt practicing one of her yoga exercises. But no, with a paint brush in hand, she was making slow, meticulous, overlapping strokes on her black shoes with white paint.

Not believing what I saw, I had to ask, "What are you doing?"

Never looking up, she answered without hesitation, "Painting my black shoes white."

"But those are your best black shoes!"

No answer came.

"Mother, why are you painting your shoes white?"

"I can't find my white shoes. They're lost."

"But why don't you use white shoe polish? Maybe you could wipe the polish off later."

"Can't find the white shoe polish. It's lost."

This was logical–lost, sometimes found, sometimes not; if not found, improvise.

I'll have to admit that when Mother left that day to demonstrate Roly Poly Sausage, she looked very official, clad from head to foot in white.

Everything will be fine, I thought, *if the paint on her shoes doesn't crack and start to peel.* But if it did, Mother would think of something.

I'VE BEEN HAD!

Finished with my daily chore of setting the table for supper, I had just sat down in the living room when the front door swung open. A form flashed past, moving through the living room, dining room, and into the kitchen. It was Mother. She just as quickly exited the kitchen and seated herself at the dining room table, digging into a heaping bowl of corn flakes.

"Mother, I put potatoes in the oven like you told me. Aren't you getting supper, or are we all having corn flakes?"

"Couldn't wait," Mother answered, munching her cold flakes.

"You act like a starving animal."

As my hamster Rory did, she shifted a wad of cereal to one side of her mouth. Her retort was, "No lunch."

"Did you leave your lunch on the bus?"

"Nope, when I got off the bus, there was this unshaven man standing on the street clutching his buttonless coat around him." She paused to resume chewing.

"And?" I coaxed, anxious to hear what the man clutching his overcoat did.

"When I started past he said, 'Nice lady, could you spare fifty cents, so's I can get a bite to eat? Ain't had nothing since yesterday.' Just having enough for bus fare home after work, I handed him my lunch."

"You mean you gave him your lunch with the ham sandwich and chocolate cake with fudge icing?"

"Yep, and do you know what he did with it?"

"I bet he gulped it down, didn't he?"

"Nope, he threw it in the trash can and went off muttering something I'd rather not repeat," Mother said, flashing me a look. "I would have fished it out, but I was already late for work. I didn't want to risk another encounter with Miss Bossy, the head nurse."

Mother, finishing her cereal, continued, "But me and Bossy locked horns anyway."

"What was it this time? Did she say your uniform looked like it had been pressed with a waffle iron? Did she accuse you of playing in-house psychiatrist by listening to the patients' problems? Or . . . ."

"No," Mother interrupted. "This time it was over the patients' trays. You would just have to have been there. Up came the trays steaming hot and giving off the aroma of baked steak, green beans, and hot coffee. It was almost more than I could stand. My rumbling stomach sounded like my big intestine was raging war against my little intestine."

I was able to identify with her predicament, because with her involved in telling the events of her day, the cooking had almost come to a standstill. I, too, was now eyeing the box of corn flakes on top of the refrigerator.

"Amid my stomach's rumblings," Mother went on, "I saw room 205's light flash. Mrs. Finnigan wanted her tray picked up. When I reached her room, the tray was untouched and heaped with all that good food plus apple cobbler with its oozing juices.

" 'Away with it,' Mrs. Finnegan said, with the flick of her wrist. 'The thought of food just chokes me.'

"She must have seen the tell-tale look of hunger in my eyes or else heard my stomach rumbling, for she said, 'If you see anything you want, help yourself. Lord knows I'm paying an arm and a leg for it in this hospital.'

" 'They'll just throw it away downstairs,' I heard myself whisper.'

" 'Sure, honey,' agreed Mrs. Finnegan. 'Just sit down in that chair behind the door and help yourself. You'll be doing me a favor. It'll keep those nurses from pestering me about not eating.'

"In my weakened condition, I couldn't fight this line of reasoning. Taking the chair behind the door, so as not to be spotted from down the hall, I had just bitten into the warm crusty roll all covered with butter when the door flew back. This was followed by the piercing voice of guess who?"

"Miss Bossy," I answered.

"Right," Mother said. "Marching straight in, she asked, 'You seen Erwin in here?' Everything was quiet. I assumed the fetal position, pressing myself against the wall in an attempt to be invisible. Shaking her head in disgust, Miss Bossy whirled to go out. That's when we made contact, eyeball to eyeball."

"Momma, what did you do?"

"Without thinking, my arm jutted out, roll in hand, and I offered, 'Would you like half of my roll Miss Bossy? They really are good.' "

"Momma!" I exclaimed, placing my hand over my mouth.

"At first Bossy had a startled look on her face. Then her expression broke into a smile, and she started laughing. 'Nobody but you, Erwin, would respond to getting caught eating from a patient's tray by trying to make me an accomplice to the crime.' "

"So you didn't get fired?"

"Nope, but I didn't get to finish my lunch either. Bossy followed me down the hall to see that the tray was placed on the food cart."

"Well, if you don't get on with supper," I warned, "Dad's going to fire you as head cook and bottle washer, and that wino on the street corner is going to have a partner begging handouts."

"After what I've been through," said Mother, "that wino will have to con someone else. I won't be had two days in a row. As for your dad, he knows when he's got a good thing going."

With that last bit of humor, we both laughed.

MOONLIGHTING

At our house, when we were in the red and Mom's part-time work was not enough to tide us over, Dad would do some moonlighting with his cohort, Jim Johnson. They did carpentry, house painting, and car repairs. They were jacks-of-all-trades.

Finally they hooked up with a landscaping concern which meant planting, spraying, and trimming trees. When the landscaping business hit a slump, say around Christmas, Dad and Jim branched out on their own.

One of their ventures, or schemes, scams or whatever, was selling Christmas trees. Their customers were a select population, the well-to-do, who availed themselves of the landscaping company's services.

Jim introduced the idea to Dad, who initially viewed it as having the stench of dishonesty. "Johnson, what idiot is going to pay fourteen bucks for a tree we're going to Sears and buy for two?"

"Vinson, good businessmen recognize it's not so much the product that makes it sell but the marketing of the product."

Dad shot Jim a doubting look.

"Visibility and convenience are factors also," Johnson continued.

"How are we going to be anymore visible and convenient at fourteen dollars than Sears is at two?"

"We're going to go right up to the door with tree in hand. You couldn't get much more visible and convenient than that, could you?"

Dad, tilting his head to the side and pressing his lips tightly together, was weighing this line of thinking. "There's still a big gap between two bucks and fourteen, Johnson!"

"If you had a suit tailor-made, you would expect to pay more than if you bought it off the rack, wouldn't you?"

"Johnson, how are you going to tailor-make a tree? Trees are God-made, not man-made."

"That's simple, Vinson. If the customer needs a fatter and taller tree, we can add on branches, and if they need a skinnier and shorter tree, we'll just take away branches."

"I guess also if the buyer wanted a stand on it, we could do that?" asked Dad, looking at Johnson questioningly.

"Sure thing," agreed Johnson. "Now how much more tailored could anything be?" Thus the partnership was formed.

Pooling their meager resources, they purchased the trees. Each man, Christmas tree in hand, would go to the prospective buyer's door. Having two trees to show allowed comparison. Of course they explained that there were more in the truck.

At this point, not only was the offer made to tailor the tree in shape and size to fit the house in question, but the name of the tree, its origin and special characteristics were tailored for this wealthy buyer. The pine became a balsam fir, not from Putnam County, but northern Canada, and these trees were guaranteed not to shed for at least six weeks.

Johnson, flashing his broad smile, would say, "Now they may eventually turn brown, but not a needle will fall."

Since Dad had given the trees a good shake when he removed them from the truck, they knew this guarantee was good until they at least got out of sight.

Dad each night at supper would describe to Mother in great detail the architectural design and fine furnishings in the homes where he and Johnson visited. Mother would shake her head in awe.

"Nadine, Johnson and I went to this one house, and all the walls in the living room were glass. I never saw anything like it."

"Snooty?" questioned Mother.

"No, the lady was real nice. She gave us cookies and coffee and bought two trees. We put stands on the trees for her."

"That was good," Mother shook her head while still weighing the integrity of this business venture.

"They're not all that nice, though," Dad rolled his eyes. "We went up to one door and asked the man if he would like to buy a fine Christmas tree."

"He said, 'Hell no!' and slammed the door in our faces. Come to find out, Mr. Goldstein was Jewish."

A look of alarm briefly swept across Mother's face at the thought of this encounter, but she managed to cover her concern by saying, "Would be like trying to sell a refrigerator to an Eskimo, I guess."

A couple of days later when Dad came home, Mother gave the appearance of being excited. "Vinson, one of your woman customers called today."

Dad beamed. "She did? Wanting another tree, is she?"

"Hardly," Mother shot back. "She claims she found a two dollar Sears' price tag in the top of her tree. She's mad as a wet hen, and I don't blame her, after she paid fourteen dollars."

Dad paled.

"When she hung up, Vinson, she said she was going to contact the Better Business Bureau or something like that."

Dad lunged for the phone to alert Johnson. During the conversation, he turned and looked full-face at Mother, "Nadine!" Mother's back stiffened when her name was called. "Johnson wants to know how the woman in South Hills got my phone number?"

Mother shrugged her shoulders and looked away. "Beats me! All I know is the two of you are going to fool around and get fined right here at Christmas time."

Dad and Johnson often talked of how the customer got the phone number. They never settled this mystery, nor did they ever attempt to sell more trees, Christmas or otherwise.

I was the only one Mother swore to secrecy that the alleged phone call never happened.

IT'S FOR THE BIRDS

"Johnson, your lawn looks like it could use some fertilizer. It's turning brown."

From inside our parked car Mother volunteered, "Well, ours is no better, Vinson. Like they always say, though, the plumber's pipes leak, the cobbler's children go barefoot and the landscaper's lawns go unfertilized . . . or something like that."

"Nadine!" After a long stare from Dad, Mother resumed working her crossword puzzle, refrained from speaking and assumed the role of a listener.

"What would perk up your lawn," Dad suggested, "is some chicken and cow manure. Probably a trailer load would do it."

"You mean spread raw manure on my lawn?"

"Sure, I use cow manure on my garden plot. Works wonders!"

"I'm game. Know anybody who has any to spare?"

"My sis Iola, down on Cow Creek, raises chickens and cows. She'll give us some."

"Well then, that's our source, but we can't throw manure loose in our cars. How will we haul it from Cow Creek up here?"

"Bill Bailey, up at the plant, has that homemade open bed trailer that hooks on the back of a car. We'll borrow it."

"Vinson, I can't believe you're this concerned with the upkeep of my lawn to go to all that trouble."

"Well, the truth is, I need some fertilizer to feed the grass that I am going to plant. So, we'll get you a load and me a load. You can have the first load."

Two days later, wearing their rubber galoshes and coveralls and equipped with shovels, Jim and Dad left for Iola's to empty the chicken house and barn of their fragrant contents.

Accomplishing this task, they returned with their dubious treasure plus a bonus of green flies.

Dad, being a man of his word, having promised Jim the first load, drove up in front of Johnson's house, unhooked the trailer from his Hudson Terraplane, and drove off—leaving Johnson and a shovel.

Bunch, Jim's wife, had not been advised of this lawn enrichment program. Her reaction was, "Oh, no! You're not leaving that pile of manure parked in front of this house."

"It's not a permanent fixture, Honey Bunch. I'm going to spread the fertilizer on the lawn first chance I get."

"No way, Jim Johnson. You couldn't walk on the lawn for a month or two without tracking manure in the house. It's unsanitary. Look at those flies. Every time I open the door a dozen swarm in."

Jim phoned Dad to explain his dilemma and to ask for some relief. "Vinson, if you take this load of manure off my hands, we won't have to make a second trip. One load will do it because Bunch says I can't dump this stuff in our yard."

Dad was so congenial and compatible that it caused suspicion that this was his plan all along. He probably figured Bunch would stop this lawn enrichment program once it came to her attention. So he drove over to Johnson's, hooked the trailer to the Hudson Terraplane, and went driving off escorted by the green flies.

Arriving in front of our house, Dad decided to get the trailer as close as he could to where the lawn had been seeded. He put the car in reverse and was backing down through the side yard when the homemade trailer came loose from the hitch. The trailer went rolling faster and faster over the hill dispersing its amber contents up into the tree branches, bushes, and onto the side of the house. The flies, being faithful to their charge, followed in pursuit.

Late in the night, Dad was gathering what he could of the manure and spreading it onto the freshly seeded area of the lawn. The next morning we were awakened to the chatter of the birds.

Mother got up to fix breakfast. In a few minutes she roused Dad and me out of bed by commenting in a droll manner, "Vinson, I didn't know you were making a bid for membership in the Audubon Society."

"What are you talking about, Nadine?"

"The Audubon Society would certainly be supportive of your effort to feed all the birds in St. Albans and adjoining areas. Look out the window."

Following her suggestion, what did we see but flock after flock of birds descending on our yard. They were attracted by the chicken feed which had dropped onto the floor of the chicken house mixing with the chicken droppings. Once attracted by the chicken feed, the birds developed a taste for grass seed and were consuming it also. Dad, exhausted by the late hours of labor from the night before, just threw his hands up and walked away from the window a beaten man.

Johnson, visiting one evening about two months after the enrichment program had been initiated, commented on the fact that grass never had come up. "Vinson, I think what would perk your lawn up is a combination of chicken and . . ."

Dad interrupted Jim before he could finish. "Just forget it, Johnson; just forget it!"

POSSUM HUNTING

Mother worked in the only hardware store in town, Leonard's, in the late thirties and early forties. Leonard's was a gathering place for men to swap hunting and fishing stories while picking up needed supplies. As Mother dusted and stocked shelves, she could not help hearing these tall tales.

When Aunt Iola, Dad's sister down on Cow Creek, let it drop in a phone conversation that Uncle Hubert had gotten, "as fine a red possum dog as could be," it was recounted that these events were set into play.

"Vinson, Hubert got a brand new possum dog, and Iola said for us to come down and go hunting."

"Nadine, I'm not about to turn you loose in the woods at night with a gun and a hunting dog—especially with Hubert and me in the same woods."

"And why not?" demanded Mother, placing her hands on her hips.

"Nadine, you've almost killed me twice fishing. Even for normal people, the chance of getting killed hunting is greater than getting killed fishing."

"Are you saying you're not normal, Vinson?"

"Not me, Nadine, you."

Mother, knowing not to be drawn into this side issue, stayed on the topic at hand, "And how did I almost get you killed fishing?"

"The time you traded your .22 rifle to Henry Ellis for a fishing boat, and you sent me out on Coal River to get it. Remember?" He questioned, looking directly into her eyes.

No answer.

"I stepped in, the bottom fell out, and I went through. I would have drowned for sure, if I hadn't caught hold of that tree root."

"Henry never did give my rifle back to make up for that old rotten boat. I bet he is still laughing up his sleeve about

50

that deal. Can you imagine a man taking advantage of a woman like that?" Mother huffed.

"Now, Nadine, about the second time you almost got me killed fishing. Nothing would do but for you to stand on that rock that jutted high over the river to do our fishing. Do you remember that?"

Silence.

"Here you were casting out and caught a pair of spectacles. From underneath that overhang within a split second of your hooking the spectacles, came a man with nostrils flared, face red, shaking his fist and using words that even I never heard before, telling me I better get my woman under control or else! He said you jerked his glasses plum off his face and nearly took his ears with them."

"How should I know that ole man Frazier was standing under that very overhang fishing? Everybody knows he's half loony," Mother answered defensively.

"Being loony would explain his expecting me to get you under control, I guess," Dad nodded.

"But everybody ought to have a third chance, Vinson."

"You mean a third chance to do your husband in, Nadine?"

"No, at fishing and hunting."

"Nadine, let's just go squirrel hunting. You do that in broad daylight, and you don't use dogs."

"That brings to mind a question I've always had about squirrels. Are gray squirrels elderly red squirrels?"

Dad's eyes rolled upward as if seeking strength from above. "No, Nadine, but that question makes me wonder even about squirrel hunting."

"Possum hunting, possum hunting," Mother insisted.

"Okay, Okay, Nadine, I'll call Hubert."

On the appointed evening, they arrived at Iola and Hubert's farm. After some struggling, Uncle Hubert managed to get the dog into the back of the car.

51

Mother stroked the drooling dog and with excitement showing in her voice asked Hubert, "Will this dog really tree a possum?"

"Yep, he'll tree anything."

Dad, anxious to get started, interrupted. "Do you know where to go to do some good possum hunting, Hubert?"

Spitting out a stream of amber tobacco juice, Hubert, a tall thin man with work-worn hands, replied, "Yep, where it's not too hard to walk. Drive back down here to where we can leave the main road, getting on that side road where Blake's old abandoned farm is. There where there are lots of persimmon trees."

"Possum do love persimmons," Mother interjected with authority.

Pulling onto the Blake farm, Dad said to Hubert, "I just don't believe that dog will tree a possum."

"Yep, he will. But, if he don't get one treed in an hour, we'll leave."

"I'm not leaving here without seeing a possum up a tree!" Mother insisted.

When let out of the car, the dog took off past the weathered gray barn heading for a thicket of persimmon trees. It wasn't three minutes until the dog started barking.

"Hubert, wonder what he's barking at?"

"He's barking at a possum, Nadine. Let's go!"

The three hunters took up through the woods in the direction of the dog. When they reached the dog, there sat a big possum in the persimmon tree. Everything was silent except for their breathing when Dad whispered, "I'm going to shoot that booger plum off there."

Caught up in the excitement Mother said, "No, I'm going to shoot him right between the eyes!"

There was an exchange between the two on whether Mother could aim good enough to hit the possum. "Right between the eyes," were her reassuring words.

Uncle Hubert got Mom positioned, so she could hit the possum in the head while Dad shone a flashlight on the critter.

"I think I got it about right," Mother said. The gun shot rang out and echoed up through the hollow into the darkness. The possum fell out of the tree with a thump.

Dad, with flashlight in hand, retrieved the body. Holding it up to examine, he looked at its head and at the rest of its body. Mother looked away.

"So, by the way, Nadine, you shot him dead center."

Mother caught up again by her sure marksmanship, said confidently, "Right between the eyes—just like I told you, huh?"

"Not unless that gunshot was so powerful that it relocated the possum's eyes. You shot the critter dead center up the hind end, Nadine."

"But, he is dead, isn't he?"

"Yep, sure is. Probably died of shock! What you need, Nadine, before we come hunting again is a class in anatomy."

PARADISE?

When Mother needed a break from cooking, washing dishes, and other activities associated with the culinary arts, she devised ways to get Dad out of the house. She might create an egg emergency by saying, "Vinson, the cake Patty wants for her birthday calls for a dozen eggs. You'll have to get some."

Nothing but fresh eggs would do—which required a trip to Aunt Iola's farm. If Dad got a late start for Cow Creek, he usually spent the night with Iola and Hubert. Mother, when convenient for her, would make sure his start was late.

When this means and all others failed to remove Dad from the scene, she would convince Doc Jackson that Dad looked peaked, which was plausible, since he had a heart condition, and that he should be admitted to the hospital for tests. Her favorite tactic, however, was to send Dad on a fishing or hunting trip which required little persuasion on her part. The following is one such incident passed on to me by my uncle.

Mother sent for a travel brochure on Waters, Michigan, a haven for hunters and fishermen, located in the northernmost part of Michigan's peninsula. When the brochure arrived, she read it with relish in order to give vivid verbal and visual descriptions of this paradise. Enticed by her presentations, given at every opportunity, Dad and Carl succumbed to the call of the wild.

Dad had hunted for years, and Carl, being a newcomer to this sport, viewed him as an expert. As Carl headed his old Chevy northward for over 500 miles, he respectfully listened to Dad's explicit instructions on firearm safety—the cleaning, loading, and unloading of guns, as well as the breaking down and carrying a gun in the field.

Second only to the discussion of hunting and the use of firearms was the topic of food. At a restaurant, Dad might order up six pancakes, sausage, two eggs, and three cups of coffee, which vanished from his plate within minutes. While paying the bill, he would shift a toothpick from one side of his mouth to the other and ask the waitress, "How far to the next good eating place?"

Carl interpreted the waitress's questioning expression as, "Something wrong with the food?" A quick glance, however, at the slick platter erased this possibility. The answer was simply that this trip pre-dated interstates and fast food places, and Dad wasn't about to put too many miles between him and food.

At the general store in Waters, where they picked up supplies and the key to their cabin, credence was given to Nadine's grandiose description of the hunting in this area. The natives told them about the abundance of ducks in the lakes near their cabin. Carl and Vinson, with duck stamp in hand, left this last outpost of human habitation to face the elements of late October.

The only diversion from the cold and miles that were being put between them and the general store was Dad's continuous detailed instruction on gun safety. Carl, listening patiently, welcomed the sight of their cabin where they were greeted by their guide, Harry, and his wife, Mrs. Farlinger, the cook, whom Nadine hired by mail.

It didn't take long to figure out that Harry, a weather-beaten man of small stature, was just not right in the head. Conversation revealed that Harry drew a small pension from the army because he had been kicked in the head by an army mule during the war. When asked, "Which war?" Harry responded, "The War of 1812."

While talking to Harry, Carl overheard Mrs. Farlinger, a huge woman who couldn't talk plain, receiving instruction from Dad on what she should prepare for breakfast. "Now could you fix us some wheatcakes?" Receiving no sign of recognition from Mrs. Farlinger, he added, "something like flapjacks."

Shaking her head she replied, "Don't know nothing about flapjacks. Make batter biscuits."

"That will be Okay. Make syrup to put on them."

"Don't know nothing about syrup. Make squint."

Dad, envisioning squint as something awful, perhaps dirty, or even immoral, looked at Carl for an explanation. Carl, equally befuddled, said, "Fix what you know. I don't give a cuss. Whatever you feed Harry will do."

Squint turned out to be a horrible sight—dark brown gravy with chunks of salt bacon and biscuits floating around in it. But by the time Dad and Uncle Carl got it, they were so hungry that it tasted good.

After taking care of eating and other necessities, Harry showed the two of them the best lake for duck hunting. Due to the abundance of marsh lands, there was a lot of underbrush called "Chintangle." It was this growth, combined with the isolation of the lakes, that made this a good habitat for ducks.

The following morning, Dad and Carl were ready at 4:30 as planned. But Harry, having the flux, wasn't. They set out alone.

Flashlights in hand, they crawled toward the lake on their bellies through the Chintangle still wet from frost. Carl, bringing up the rear, caught the blunt of the Chintangle across his face as Dad plowed hurriedly ahead, leaving Carl badly scratched, cold, and wet by the time they reached the blinds they built the day before.

With Dad giving directions on how they should shoot simultaneously, they waited in the cold damp air for what seemed an hour. The only thing moving was the mist coming off the lake and the vapor as they breathed.

The silence was broken by Carl, "Vinson, I don't think there's a duck about." Dad shared Carl's suspicions but reiterated if anything should appear that they shoot together.

Daybreak bore proof to their fears—no ducks! "Do you reckon there are any ducks in these parts, Carl?"

"The only thing I know is that I'm half frozen."

They had just about decided to give up when Carl cocked his ear at something which sounded like a rush of wind. "Hold it, Vinson. Hear that?"

"Yeah! Sounds like an airplane, but not quite."

With their eyes fixed skyward, they saw coming into view what appeared to be a cloud. A cloud which as it came nearer broke into small parts and took wing. It now looked as if all the ducks in the world were converging on that spot. Carl sat motionless muttering, "I don't believe it; I don't believe it."

Shaking from cold and nervous exhilaration as they watched the ducks land on the other end of the lake, they feared the ducks might never get within shooting range. Suddenly a small group broke away from the rest and headed in their direction. They counted sixteen. Carl and Vinson agreed that it was the prettiest sight they ever saw.

Dad instructed Carl not to talk anymore. "Those ducks are almost on us," he warned; "When they come within range, we'll fire together."

The ducks swam closer and closer. Carl was thinking that Dad was never going to signal when Dad whispered, "Okay! Okay!" and aimed his twelve gauge with its twenty-eight inch barrel.

Carl got off five quick shots with his Browning automatic. A pair of ducks dropped and floated toward them as the others took flight. Carl contained his cry of victory when he heard muttering and complaining coming from behind Dad's blind. A more dejected man Carl had never seen. Shoulders slumped, lower lip protruding and hands dangling across his knees, Dad sat with his head down.

"Vinson, what's the matter?" Silence. "Vinson, you Okay?" Silence. "Vinson! What's wrong?"

"I didn't get off a shot, nary a one."

"Did she jam on you?"

"Nope."

"What happened?"

"You know, for safety, I said not to load till we got here?"

Carl nodded.

"Well, as far as I was concerned, everything including the ducks was safe."

"Vinson, you mean . . ."

"That's right. I forgot to load. Carl, promise me you won't say a word about this to anyone back home."

"We'll just forget it, Vinson, and what will help us to forget," Carl said with a chuckle, "is Mrs. Farlinger's squint and biscuits waiting back at the cabin."

Dad, gathering together his gear, commented, "Nadine sure hired us a couple of winners, didn't she? When we get home, I'm going to tell her that if this is her idea of paradise, I'd sooner shoot for hell!"

THE PACKARD

"Bunch, do you think we can get rid of Vinson and Jim this long change? They will have five days off between midnight and day shift. I don't know if I can stand Vinson puttering around and getting underfoot. Besides, he needs a rest."

"Don't worry, Nadine. Those two will cook up somewhere to go without our coaching."

This time, Mother, taking Bunch's advice and going on faith—things hoped for but not yet seen—let Dad do the maneuvering.

"Nadine, Jim wants me to go fishing over to Chesapeake Bay, but I guess I don't have the money."

"Suppose not, Vinson, with insurance due."

"Jim said he had a cheap place to stay. It will only cost twenty dollars. Split that, and it would be ten dollars each."

Mother, seemingly engrossed in hemming my skirt, answered, "I think you're right, Vinson. Two into twenty is ten."

Following a brief pause, Dad said, "I could go down to Sis's and dig some potatoes and get eggs. Jim and I'll be catching plenty of fish. Gasoline is only twenty-five cents a gallon." He pulled out a pencil and began figuring.

Mother, trying to appear cool, added slowly and thoughtfully, "There's stuff in the refrigerator for lunches on the way over."

"I don't want to empty the refrigerator. I don't have much cash to leave here."

"Don't worry. As long as I've got fingers to dial the phone and feet to carry me to the bus stop, Patty and I will make it."

A disturbed look shot across Dad's face. Perhaps Mother had said too much.

"Which car are you taking?" She phrased the question to indicate the trip was no longer a wish but a fact.

"Jim's."

"You mean that twenty-year-old Packard that looks like it has a case of acne, with the burlap sack covering the busted windows?"

"It'll do fine. Jim and I are fair mechanics. Besides, it will save putting a thousand miles on my car."

While Dad went to the farm for food, Jim went to the junkyard to get a floor mat to cover the rust holes in the Packard's floor. The car produced oil vapors and smoke which seeped up through the holes, giving Dad a headache. It was hoped that the floor mat would correct this small problem, because there were bigger ones. The voltage regulator was on the blink, and the battery was run down. In short, the car had to be pushed to start.

However, minor details like this could not stand in the way of their salt-water fishing. Jim and Dad, dressed in their best sports clothes—white shirts and khaki pants—having completed all their errands, drove off.

Somewhere in Virginia the voltage regulator became more erratic. Jim and Dad watched it in silence. Finally, Jim said, "Vinson, if my memory serves me right, we'll be coming up on a junkyard soon. With luck, we can pick up a good used voltage regulator and scrap this one."

Dad agreeing, they stopped. While Jim made the purchase, Dad removed the hood to get at the old regulator, looking all the while for a spot to change his good clothes.

"Here, Vinson, hold the hood up," Dad complied.

Using the hood for a screen, Jim stood between it and the car and dropped his pants. "You're going to change clothes right here on the side of the highway, Johnson?"

"Don't see any better place," Jim replied.

So Dad took his turn behind the hood. Clad in their grubbies, the two worked quickly, switching the regulators.

"Now, what are we going to do with this old one, Johnson? We can't leave it here on the side of the road. All we need is to get fined for littering."

A gleam entered Johnson's eyes. "I'll tell you what; I'll take the old one back and tell the junk dealer it's the one we just bought, and it doesn't work. Maybe we'll get our five dollars back."

Dad shook his head in disbelief that Jim could do such a thing, when Jim reminded him they were short of money.

Not seeming to soothe Dad's conscience sufficiently, Jim added, "I just noticed, Vinson, that with the hood off, the smoke and vapors will go straight up rather than through the floor. I'll nonchalantly leave the hood in the junkyard. It's worth something."

With the five dollars back in their pocket, dressed in their grubbies and wearing five-o-clock shadows, the pair set out again in the Packard, minus the hood.

As they drove deeper and deeper into the Blue Ridge Mountains, dark set in and the car lights began to dim—the rebuilt regulator was on its way out. "Seems the junkman got the last laugh, Johnson. Now what are we going to do?"

"We're going to share."

"Share what with whom, Johnson? There's nothing on this isolated stretch except deer and bear."

"I'll show you." Johnson hit the gas and zoomed around the mountains, cutting curves in half until he caught up with the only other car on the stretch. Johnson then flipped off the headlights. "See, we are sharing the lights from that nice gentleman up ahead."

The plan worked for about thirty miles, at which point the nice gentleman must have gotten a good look at the two characters trailing him. No doubt they meant to rob him. Why else would this pair drive without lights on this isolated road? These must have been the driver's thoughts because he increased his speed. The groaning Packard, squealing on the turns, offered a gallant chase until it began heating up, and Jim was forced to drop back.

"I see a gas station at the foot of the mountain. See the lights, Johnson? We'd best get water before this car explodes."

They could only reason that the station attendant mistook the burlap-winged, pock-marked Packard with smoke pouring from its front and rear as a UFO descending the mountain. For when Dad and Jim pulled to the pumps, all sign of life had vanished. Nobody could be roused.

Even if the attendant had locked himself indoors and, peering out, perceived this smoking heap before him to be an automobile rather than a UFO, it was unlikely that he would have admitted the bearded, greasy-faced, raggedy pair pounding on his station door.

Jim and Dad, not being bashful, helped themselves to water and drove off into the night, arriving at their destination late. The fish were biting, and the stay made the trip worth all the hassle. Whether it made up for the return trip is the next question.

Staying to the last minute, Jim and Dad cut their time to return close. The trip went smoothly until once again, deep in the Blue Ridge Mountains—where Dad said that if there was to be any socializing it would be with a six-point deer or a black bear, the Packard caught on fire. The generator, over charging, sent flames so high that Johnson could not see out the windshield.

Eyes wide and knuckles white from gripping the seat, Dad yelled, "Stop the car, Johnson! You're going to get us both burned up!"

Obliging, Johnson pulled over. Checking the generator while Dad stood at a distance, Johnson spotted the source of the fire as the insulation around the generator. He propped the points apart with cardboard. Now the generator was not charging at all.

Giving the car a shove, Dad and Jim jumped in and took off. Dad, looking out the window, could see the flames still burning. "Aren't you going to put the fire out, Johnson?"

"No, Vinson, I'm just going to let it burn out."

Dad watched in dismay, but indeed the flames subsided.

Exhausted from all this anxiety, he drifted off to sleep, only to be awakened by Johnson's voice. "Vinson, the car is heating up and there's not a station for miles. You'll have to give up your jug of ice water."

Pulling off the road, the two got out to check the radiator. It was evident that the grill was bent, cutting off the radiator's flow of air. Dad, no longer concerned about littering, ripped off the grill and tossed it over the hill as Johnson poured the precious ice water into the thirsty, sputtering radiator.

Back on the road, convinced nothing else could happen, Dad's thoughts turned to food. "Buddy, in Lexington there's a restaurant that makes the best beef stew you ever stuck a tooth in. It's a dandy! We can just stop there and eat, can't we?"

Johnson never responded. He had, as he said later, a forced option—to get home with that car before dark.

Johnson drove fifty miles per hour through Lexington. Dad's mouth was watering just thinking about the stew. He leaned out the window as the long anticipated restaurant came into view and went out of view in a flash. Pointing, he said, "There-it-was!" With his patience tried and stomach empty, he turned and looked at Jim.

"Johnson, you won't stop to let a man eat or go to the bathroom. I always end up starved and constipated on these trips."

"Why don't you drink yourself some prune juice?" Jim asked, trying to change the subject from the restaurant.

Dad yelled back, "Why? You wouldn't let a man stop. I'd either be plugged up or messed up."

Hearing the report of this trip, Mother was concerned that Dad would never go on another. But upon asking, she was told that as soon as the burlap on the Packard's windows was mended and another hit could be made on the junkyard, come the next long change, the two would be off and running again.

THREE FOR THE ROAD

The next long change was approaching about the last of September when "Spots", a type of fish good for eating, were plentiful in Chesapeake Bay. With Mom's encouraging words, "Better go when you can—before bad weather," Jim and Dad planned their next fishing trip.

They talked with such enthusiasm to the fellows at the plant about the fine time on their last venture that it whetted others' appetites. One guy, Bill Jones, said he would go and drive his new car. This was fine with Jim and Dad. This would give the old Packard a well deserved rest.

Bill was surprised by the projected inexpensive cost of the trip—one might even say skeptical. However, Dad and Jim assured him if there was anything not covered or provided which Bill felt he could not live without that they would show him how he could.

Bill had never been salt-water fishing and was anxious to get started. So the three left directly from the plant, following their last midnight shift, with Bill driving, Jim riding shotgun, and Dad riding in the back seat to get some "shuteye."

But no sleep was gotten. Bill left the parking lot with gusto, building up to ninety-five miles an hour in no time flat. Dad bolted upright in his seat, wide eyed and speechless as he watched the zigzag fence along the side of the highway give the appearance of straightening out due to the speed of the car. Bill was also straightening out curves by driving in the middle of the road.

Upon cresting one hill, an old man wearing a wide-brimmed hat and carrying a bag of groceries came into view. Hearing the fast approaching car, he looked over his shoulder, dropped the bag by the side of the road, jumped the fence, ran up the hill and clung tenaciously to a handy sassafras tree.

"What's wrong with him? Is he crazy?" asked Bill glancing in his rear view mirror where the man quickly became but a speck.

"No, no, we're the crazy ones," answered Dad emphatically. "If we had come through there sideways, we would have wiped him out. Neither one of us is ready to meet our maker yet."

This incident slowed Bill down for a while, but as the morning progressed, so did the speed. Then came that dreaded sound—a police siren. "Oh my gosh," Dad said. "Pull over; they've got us now."

"I'll do the talking," volunteered Jim as he and Bill got out of the car and walked that long walk toward a policeman waiting to fine them.

Dad just looked down shaking his head. Several minutes passed before he looked up and saw Jim showing the officer his plant security guard identification. This was followed by more talking. Finally Jim and Bill returned to the car.

"How much was the fine?" Dad asked anxiously.

"No fine," answered Jim. "He just said to slow down until we get out of his State."

Jim saw Dad's face turning crimson. "What's wrong, Vinson? You disappointed because we didn't get fined."

"Well, we were breaking all limits, Johnson. Here we get caught, and you slick talk the patrolman. I guess he apologized by saying, 'I'm sorry I stopped you.'"

"Vinson, don't get all tore up over it. Think of the money we saved," Jim responded.

Not long after this, Dad had to endure further disappointment. The sit down dinner he was looking forward to had to be eaten on the wing.

While the car was being serviced, Dad hurried into the adjoining restaurant to check the menu, which looked like it doubled as a flyswatter. He was anticipating a big bowl of pinto beans and hunk of cornbread when Johnson breezed in and said to the cook, "Wrap up six hamburgers to go."

Seeing Dad's look of dismay, Johnson explained that if they did not keep moving, they would be unable to find a parking place at Ocean View's City Park. If they tried to sleep in the car anywhere else, they would be breaking the vagrancy law. Dad certainly did not want that.

By eating their hamburgers, fries, and coffee as best they could in a moving car, the three fishermen did arrive and get a place in the park. Exhausted from working all night and driving all day, they decided, without quibbling, that Bill would sleep in the front seat, Dad in the back seat, and Jim in the floor over the hump. After removing only their shoes, the front and back doors swung open, and out popped six feet.

The three slept so soundly that they were unaware until the next morning of the swarm of mosquitoes biting a band around all six legs in the gap between their pants and socks. But this little inconvenience, along with having to walk sideways as a result of sleeping in such cramped quarters, did not dampen their good time—fishing, seeing a beached sea turtle the size of a car and touring a battleship. After all, battleships and sea turtles did not venture up Cow Creek, Scary Creek or even Kanawha River.

When Dad was working four-to-twelve shift or had a day off, I often awoke to the murmur of Mother and Dad's talking during breakfast. This usually gave me a cozy feeling, but the conversation I heard one morning shook my security and added a new dimension to our family.

"Don't sit there smiling like a Chessy cat, Vinson. I'm so embarrassed."

"Just didn't think the old man still had it, did you?"

"Vinson, stop that. How can I face Christine, Bunch, Lillian, and my other friends."

"I don't know why you're so upset. You are a married woman!"

"A forty-five-year-old married woman who's pregnant. It's not normal to be having a baby after forty."

"Nobody expects you to be normal, Nadine."

I heard a coffee cup tap up against a plate as it was being placed back on the table. "True, I always wanted four children and we only have one." Mother's voice drifted dreamily off.

Dad assumed the anxious role that Mother abandoned.

"Now don't get carried away, Nadine. One boy will be a plenty."

At these words, hot tears sprang to my eyes. I was gripped by the fear of being replaced. Dad had always wanted a boy. Had I not heard him say that if he had a boy he could help mow the lawn. I never had to share affection or attention. My mother was betraying me. I lay in bed immersed in self pity. How could she do this? I'd run away. That would hurt them.

These thoughts were interrupted by Mother's coaxing voice. "You sleepyhead, get up. I've fixed you pancakes with some of Iola's butter and maple syrup."

She did not seem to notice that there was no answer. I wanted her to notice, but she returned to the dining room. I'd have to go in there if she was ever going to know I was angry.

Mother resumed her place at the end of the table to drink her second cup of coffee and to keep me company. I was looking as mean as I could, but she just went on chattering. How frustrating! I had never tried to be angry with my mother before.

"Daddy's going to the farm. You and I can go to big town to buy you a bathing suit. Summer is just around the corner. We'll eat at the Quarrier Diner, and there is a Shirley Temple movie." She went on and on while I was dying inside.

"Instead of a bathing suit for me, you better start buying baby things." I broke in sharply. Then I folded my arms and glared out the window, not wanting our eyes to meet.

Mother sat quietly and thoughtfully. She knew I overheard, which ruined her plans to tell me the news under favorable conditions. "December is a long time away. Meantime summer is coming, and you need a bathing suit." With this, she began clearing dishes. Then she stopped—reached over and patted my head. "Momma and Daddy love you, and we always will. You can never be replaced." Those were the words I hungered for. I needed to hear them again and again, and I did.

Mother's proportions slowly began to balloon. Her 5' 2" frame carried 180 pounds at nine months. She always laughed when I said she looked like a Studebaker. As the summer progressed, and it got hotter, Mother spent more time in our cool basement. Air-conditioned small homes like ours were unheard of. We did not even have a fan.

When she returned from another visit to Doctor Lovejoy, I heard her telling Dad, "Vinson, here I sit looking like I swallowed a watermelon at five months, and these young things come waltzing in, ready to deliver, looking like they swallowed a grape."

69

"But they're not going to have the honor of being the token senior citizen at their school's PTA meeting either," Dad would say reassuringly.

"We'll probably be tagged as the poor child's grandparents," was Mother's answer.

She, including me in as many plans as possible, was leading me through these nine months very well, when suddenly I regressed. One of my schoolmates told me, "I heard my mother talking about your mother having a baby and that at her age she could die."

I was numbed. This possibility had never crossed my mind. Again I became sullen. Mother, quickly picking up on my mood change, came to my room one evening carrying a baby-name book and said, "Since this is going to be your brother or sister, Daddy and I think you should choose the name."

Clutching the book to my chest, I managed to get out between sobs, "Could you die having a baby, Momma? Jan said you could."

"I don't intend to. Dr. Lovejoy is the best specialist I could find. Don't worry; just pick a name. You have to be my helper."

A shadow of doubt still lingered, but my thoughts were consumed with finding the perfect name—a pretty girl's name and an ugly boy's name. After much deliberation, I decided on Cynthia Elaine for my sister and Huey Luchian or, on second thought, Huey Luchian Oscar for a boy.

When Mother's friends came calling and started a conversation such as, "Nadine, you didn't have to go to this extreme to prove there is sex after forty," I would volunteer the names I had picked. Upon hearing the boy's name, they rolled their eyes at Mother as if saying, "You wouldn't, Nadine." She would just smile.

At this, I added, "Remember, all the baby gifts should be pink." They were, every single one.

When Mother's time came, she had a long hard labor. I stayed with Mrs. Morris who broke the news that I was a sister of a healthy boy. After being assured Mother was fine, I managed to keep a calm exterior, but inside my head Rumplestiltskin was jumping around shouting, "I have the name! I have the name!"

Dad, proud as punch, took me to the hospital to visit Mother.

"Here is my little girl I've been telling you about," Mother said to the nurse as I walked over to give Mother a hug.

I touched what had once been her firm protruding stomach to find that now it was very soft but not yet flat. "You are not a Studebaker," I teased.

"No, but now you have a baby to name."

The nurse was waiting with poised pencil and official papers in hand.

"Huey Luchian Oscar," I said with authority.

The nurse's pencil did not move, but her jaw dropped.

"Patty, that's fine, but I think you should see something before you name it. Don't you?" Mother questioned.

"That's right," agreed the nurse. "Let's go look at your new baby." She ushered me to the nursery past eyes questioning my presence. I looked through the glass at all the tiny forms, some crying, some sleeping, and some looking around. "That's your baby here up next to the glass," said the nurse. "Is it still Huey Luchian Oscar?"

Mesmerized by what came out of Mother's stomach, I shook my head no.

With a sigh of relief, the nurse pressed another baby-name book into my hand. From this I chose the proper name for my new brother—David, which means beloved and for the middle name, Vinson, after my father.

THE INTERRUPTED SILENCE

Spring affects people in different ways. Some think of gardening, some spring cleaning and others enjoying the beauty that nature affords. My mother's fancy turned to flea markets, garage sales (bug sales she called them), and auctions.

When I was a young girl, the months of April, May and June were never dull around my house. Familiar pieces of furniture would disappear only to be replaced by unfamiliar pieces which exhibited dire need of repair. Even as a youngster, I was perceptive enough to recognize that my mother had neither the gift for bartering nor for buying and selling. By surveying the newly acquired furnishings at the end of June, it did not take an economic expert to recognize that when buyer met seller and the bartering was completed, someone other than Mother was getting the better end of the deal.

My father's tolerance for Mother's annual experiments with the free enterprise system grew very thin at times. I always had nervous expectations of some kind of a violent eruption from him. This expectation was never realized, but it almost was.

When I went to the dining room for breakfast one Saturday, Mother's absence was evident. She was not there with her usual inquiry about what I would be having for breakfast and my plans for the day. In fact, I seemed to be the only one about.

Then, I heard the bathroom water faucet cut on, and glancing across the dining room table, I saw a plate with remnants of drying egg and toast. This told me that Dad had eaten breakfast and was in the bathroom getting ready for bed. He was working the midnight shift or what we referred to as the "Hoot Owl Shift."

I got myself a glass of milk and flipped through the morning paper. The sounds coming from the bathroom were familiar because Dad never deviated from his routine when getting ready for a day of hibernation.

His toiletry consisted of bathing, putting on his pajamas and removing his teeth to soak in a glass. This glass was kept in the medicine cabinet. So whenever I opened the cabinet, the teeth gave the appearance of smiling at me.

Next, Dad would pass through the dining room and go upstairs. He slept upstairs during the day to escape the household noises. He stopped only long enough to announce that he was ready for bed and would not be getting up until five that evening for supper. I knew that Dad was true to his word. Once he retired upstairs during the day, he never got up until exactly 5:00 p.m.

The pattern held true. Drinking my milk, I could hear his bare feet going across the wooden floors which squeaked back in response to his weight. Then came silence. Fifteen minutes passed before I felt my body tense. Putting my glass of milk down, I listened closely. Did I hear bare feet coming back across the floors? Yes! There was now no doubt because the footsteps were more pronounced than usual.

The steps were coming closer and now downstairs. Suddenly, with a great deal of force, the door was flung open and there stood my father. His jaws sagged from the absence of teeth, his arms were folded firmly across his stomach, and he was shaking his head in disbelief.

"What's wrong?" I asked.

"That woman has sold my bed," he said. Turning without another word, he proceeded back up the stairs. This time, I followed. There on the bedroom floor was a boxspring and mattress made up as if they indeed were placed upon a bed, but there was no bed.

Without a word, Dad lowered his body to the floor, crawled onto the mattress, fluffed the pillow, and pulled the covers around him.

I, in turn, silently stole away down the steps. Nothing more was said about the missing bed. I will admit, however, that from that day to this I have wondered what transpired in those fifteen minutes of silence, between the time my dad discovered the missing bed and his return downstairs.

SOCIAL CRISIS

David, my younger brother, Mother and I sat on the sofa like birds lined up on an electric wire ready to fly south. We were waiting for Dad to get dressed. This was a switch—he usually waited on us.

Mother kept checking the clock. "What on earth could be taking your dad so long? He knows that weddings and funerals always start on time, and it is rude to be late."

She had just finished her observation on social etiquette when Dad walked in. He had on his only suit, which was tailor made, and a shirt which had been laundered at the Chinese laundry, so the collar would be starched just so-so. He only wore his "Sunday go to meeting clothes" to church services. So having only one suit was no problem.

As he came around the corner, I felt my usual pride in his appearance. But once he came into full view, I felt David nudge me in the ribs and heard Mother clear her throat to speak. "Vinson, your socks don't match."

"I know that, Nadine. But why did you notice that little detail so quickly?"

"Because Vinson, you don't have any trousers on. You are standing there in your boxer shorts. So, I couldn't fail to notice your socks don't match."

David and I started to giggle. Dad ignored us. "Why do you think I am standing here all dressed up with the exception of my trousers?"

"You don't want to get your pants wrinkled, so you are going to keep them on the hanger until we get to the church," Mother suggested.

Dad's face reddened. "I wouldn't be strutting around in my boxer shorts for that reason. My suit trousers are missing, Nadine. I've looked everywhere for them."

"I just picked your suit up at the cleaners. It was all wrapped up in plastic. Your trousers had to be hanging with your jacket and vest."

"Well, the trousers are not on the hanger."

After some thought Mother said, "The cleaners must have forgotten to put the trousers with the vest and jacket. I'll call them now, and we can pick them up on the way to the funeral."

"Today is Sunday, and the cleaner is closed, Nadine."

"Oh, that's right." She glanced at the clock again to verify what we already knew. Time had not stopped and indeed was moving on. "Patty, David, and I can go to the funeral without you. We'll sign your name on the register, and nobody will know you did not attend."

"Of course they'll know. It's my only brother's funeral. Don't you think my mother and father would notice the absence of their now only living son?"

Mother, recognizing this as a crisis situation, went into action. "We'll just have to find you some trousers to wear," she announced.

David, Mother, and I darted off into different directions to find a pair of trousers, knowing that time was pressing in upon us. Closet doors slammed, hamper lids banged, footsteps were heard rushing up and down to the laundry.

Mother was the first to return to the living room where Dad sat leaning over resting his head in his hands, not seeming to know what to expect.

Mother, beaming proudly, held up a neatly pressed pair of pants.

"Where," Dad asked, "did those pants come from? They're not mine."

"They're Mr. Hale's."

"What are you doing with our neighbor's pants, Nadine?" His face turned a shade darker.

76

"I borrowed them, so you would have something to wear."

"You mean I'm wearing borrowed trousers which don't match my jacket and are probably an inch too long and two inches too big around the waist to my brother's funeral?"

Mother's only answer was to hand Dad the trousers.

"Well, at least I won't be arrested for indecent exposure," he mumbled as he slipped the trousers on.

"And with them hanging down on the ground like that nobody will notice your socks don't match," I offered.

Mother grabbed me by the arm and quickly ushered me out the door, mumbling reassuring phrases: "Life is not perfect. These things happen sometimes. We just have to make do. Only those who are adaptable can survive in today's stress-filled world."

Glancing over my shoulder as Mother dragged me along toward the car, I witnessed an uncomfortable silence in a man whose adaptability was wearing mighty thin.

DOING FOR OTHERS

The aroma of mashed potatoes, baked steak, fried apples and hot rolls beckoned David, Dad, and me to the table. Here, Mother was putting on the finishing touches—a round cake of butter with a pattern of acorn clusters on top. This familiar pattern gave proof that it was from Aunt Iola's.

Initially there was little talk, just the passing of plates. As our stomachs filled, however, conversation increased. The topic was politics, on which I thrived. Dad did most of the talking. We did most of the listening.

My listening was soon distracted when, from the corner of my eye, I saw David's hand edging toward the last roll on the platter. "David, you've had three rolls; that one is mine."

"Only two," he said holding up two fingers.

"You had one plain, one with butter, and one with butter and jelly."

David rolled his brown eyes and conceded.

Dad stopped talking and waited as David and I settled the roll controversy. He meant to have undivided attention when he spoke. Mother, having heard all this before, started clearing the table. A quick inventory showed extra food. "I'll fix Mrs. Scott a supper plate. Patty, you can take it over while it's still hot."

"Oh, do I have to?" I questioned without expecting an answer.

Mrs. Scott, a widow lady in our neighborhood, according to rumor, had been duped out of her inheritance by a religious cult. Now she existed on a small pension. We shared food when we could. Dad picked up her government commodities for her each month, and many a night I heard the telephone ring followed by Mother's going to Mrs. Scott's.

The next morning I would ask if Mrs. Scott were sick, and Mother would say, "Yes" or "Mrs. Scott was only scared and needed company." Once it had been another neighbor who had died, and Mother readied her for the undertaker by washing and changing her clothes.

I did not like going to Mrs. Scott's, because it left me with a sad feeling, knowing she had to live alone with only her dog for company. If I complained too much, though, I knew Dad would retell the story of the little girl he encountered while he and Johnson were delivering Christmas baskets: "You should be ashamed Patricia, you don't know how lucky we are. There are so many living up against hard circumstances right in this town. Why I went to this one house where there was a girl your age lying on a bare mattress in the floor. Her little jaw was all red and swollen out to here." He would hold his cupped hand about one inch away from his jaw to demonstrate. "Her Mother had put Red Devil Lye inside the kid's cavity to kill the pain." He would then shake his head.

"Have you ever?" Mother would join in the head shaking. "Good thing Bunch got that child to the dentist."

Since this story made me feel sadder than a visit to Mrs. Scott's, I would comply by "fetching" the food.

Mother, never prone to dwell on sadness when left on her own, told a lighter side of Dad and Johnson's Christmas project.

For several Christmases Johnson and Dad had gone door to door bumming canned goods for the needy. The names of the recipients of the bushel baskets of food were gotten from local grocery stores. After gathering the food, sorting a can of beans here, tuna there, and six cans of milk for the families with children, then loading the baskets into a car, it would be past dark by the time the actual deliveries took place.

Dad and Johnson, this particular time, had gone to a row of shanties down by the tracks behind the feed store. Going separate ways carrying bushel baskets, Dad finished first.

79

He was standing on the edge of the road smoking a cigarette, when quick as a flash he found himself staring down the barrel of a revolver held by a young police officer.

"That's him! That's him, officer!" Dad, not daring to turn his head, just shifted his eyes in the direction of the voice. He saw silhouetted in one of the shanty doorways a fleshy woman, pointing her finger right at him. "That there is the peeping Tom I been reporting to you for weeks."

"I can tell you don't belong in this neck of the woods, Mister," came the officer's voice.

"No, sir, no, sir, you're right, but I'm innocent."

"That is the standard reply," snapped the policeman. "Go on, I'm in a listening mood. You better be in a talking mood."

Dad, hearing doors opening and gruff voices of the men folk, agreed. "I'm down here giving away food and money, sir."

"I think I've heard this one before," said the officer. "Which one are you—Friar Tuck or Robin Hood? And I guess you were peeping in all the windows looking for Maid Marian."

Dad thought he saw a man pass through a yard with a shotgun. *Where could that Johnson be now?* he wondered. "I'm Friar Tuck. I mean Vinson Erwin," he stammered; "I wasn't peeping."

The policeman, sensing mounting tension, nudged Dad toward the police car as the fleshy woman yelled, "If you don't know what to do with this peeper now that you caught him, we'll show you."

Dad was in the process of saying, "Look, I've two kids and a wife—Nadine. You might know her. Might even be a cousin. She has a cousin that's a fireman."

Then the policeman's attention shifted to a man running down the muddy road whispering, "Vinson."

"That no doubt is Robin Hood," said the policeman.

"No, no," corrected Dad, "that is Johnson. It's me, Johnson, here with the policeman."

Johnson, identification in hand, quickly bridged the gap between the officer and himself by flashing his DuPont security guard identification. This was followed by his verification that he and Dad were indeed delivering food baskets. He then smooth-talked the officer into checking out their car, which still contained some food baskets. All of this confirmed that the officer had made a false assumption.

The policeman knew the three of them had better make a hasty departure void of explanation. "Get in your car and follow me," he directed. With lights flashing and Johnson and Vinson in hot pursuit, they exited the neighborhood.

Mother always got a great deal of amusement out of recounting this story. I think it was because she could not imagine anyone mistaking Dad for a peeper. That Dad, who tried to keep a low profile, was escorted out of a neighborhood by a police cruiser just put the icing on the cake for her.

REALITY

"I swear. I'll have to peel a hundred of these little potatoes to get enough for a mess of mashed potatoes. They're about the size of marbles—a steelie or taw anyway. Your dad still thinks we're in the middle of the depression, digging these culls for me to cook," Mother complained.

I passively watched as her childlike hands grasped the small paring knife which fit them well. As a sculptor, she removed the muddy brown peelings to reveal the white meat of the potatoes. I sat at the opposite end of the dining room table, drinking one of the chilled Cokes Mama always kept hidden in the lettuce crisper just for me. I was daydreaming about the movie she and I had seen the night before, *Father of the Bride*. This prompted my asking, "Mama, did you have any boyfriends before Daddy?"

"Of course I did. After all, I was thirty-one when I married."

"Was there anybody special before Daddy?" I asked, leaning forward anticipating the revelation of sordid details of unquenched love.

"Well, I'll never forget Henry," Mama answered as she stopped peeling.

Really? What was special about Henry?" I prodded.

"He always brought me an O'Henry candy bar when he came calling."

"Is that the only reason you remember Henry?"

Mama's peeling resumed as she nodded in the affirmative.

"Cousin Esther told me Preacher Myers said, right from the pulpit, that he saw you down on your knees looking in a manhole for a man. Is that true?"

Mama smiled at that remark, "Reverend Myers liked to tease me about waiting so long to get married; that's all. I was just selective. You know, the man you marry will be the father of your children. So you can't just marry anybody. It's like breeding horses."

"I'm not a horse," I retorted.

"I didn't mean you were, Patty. It's just, if you want a great racehorse, you don't breed with a plowhorse, but a stallion."

"Dad is a stallion?"

"Well, he is clean-cut, bright, works hard, doesn't drink, and is honest."

In my mind this did not qualify one as a "stallion," but I refused to get hung up on this point. "Mama, you wear a plain silver wedding band. Where is your engagement ring?"

"You have your elbows on it," was her quick response.

Lifting both elbows, I saw nothing but the dining table.

Noting my expression, Mom went on, "I traded my ring for this dining room suite when we moved into this house."

"How unromantic. You traded your diamond engagement ring for this?" I asked, gesturing toward each piece of the dining room suite.

"We needed something to eat on more than I needed a diamond."

Trying to get back into the romantic spell that *Father of the Bride* had cast wasn't easy after being told that you picked your mate based on the principles of horse breeding and used your diamond for horse trading, so to speak. "Mama, did you wear a filmy white wedding dress and veil like Elizabeth Taylor's?"

Mother paused again in her relentless peeling, and a far away look came into her eyes as she answered, "No, I wore a baby blue crepe dress with a white organdy collar trimmed in lace, and my veil was a matching blue pillbox hat. Vinson wore his pinstripe suit and vest. Of course his shirts always were starched just so. Had them done at the Chinese laundry, you

83

know. Now, Ching was not very bright, but he could launder real well."

"Why do you say Ching wasn't bright?"

"He was always showing me his newest baby's picture."

"So?"

"So, he had been living in the United States for at least five years when I first met him, and his wife, having all these babies, lived in China."

Hearing this, I pondered Uncle Carl's observation, "It rarely takes nine months for the first baby but always for the second and those that follow."

Trying to get back to the subject, I asked, "You were a June bride, weren't you?"

"Wrong! Vinson and I married on January the tenth."

"Why that date?"

"Simple, Aunt Mandy said it was bad luck to marry on the thirteenth."

"Wait," I countered, "I believe you skipped a chapter. Why not June the tenth?"

Mother, switching into her selective listening mode, heard only the part of the question she wished to respond to, and after a while I felt lucky for the crumbs of knowledge willingly given.

"I worked at Leonard's Hardware, and Vinson had just gotten hired at DuPont. We both had the thirteenth off, but as I said, Aunt Mandy thought that wasn't proper. Since we both also had January the tenth free, we took Reverend Myers to Catlettsburg, Kentucky and got married."

"Now wait, Mother, after all, by my calculations you were thirty-one. You and Dad were born the same year, 1908, so it wasn't as if you were under age and had to go across the state line to marry. Why Catlettsburg?"

"In West Virginia, there was a blood test and a three-day waiting period. In Kentucky, on the other hand, we could cut the red tape and tie the knot in one day."

My parents' wedding just did not have the romantic elements of the movie, *Father of the Bride*, so I kept probing for romance instead of the practical, practical, practical answers that I kept getting. "What was the hurry, or did you and Dad have a social disease, so you were avoiding the blood test?"

"Don't be silly, Patricia." Mom only used "Patricia" when her patience began to wear. "Vinson and I had been courting for four years. When he got his job at DuPont and was so happy, I knew that I had better strike while the iron was hot." A blush rushed to her face upon realizing the possible connotation of her words. She then speeded up the explanation. "Anyway, I asked Reverend Myers to go to Kentucky with Vinson and me. Your Dad insisted that only Preacher Myers could perform the ceremony."

"Oh, Reverend Myers married you and Dad?"

"No, he was the witness. He was not licensed in the State of Kentucky. I wanted everything legal you know."

From experience, I filled in the missing parts for Mother. "Dad assumed Reverend Myers would marry you in Catlettsburg, so he had to miss only one day of work. Right? But you knew all along that Myers could only witness, so you kidnapped him and made other arrangements for a licensed minister in Kentucky. Right?"

She shrugged, "Well, your Dad never was one for details. After Reverend Myers had rearranged his schedule to accompany us, and we were there, and all, we did find another minister. His wife sang and played the piano. It was real nice. I had a corsage of white carnations and everything."

"I suppose the stallion bought that."

"Of course," Mom replied.

Still looking for romance, I continued, "I bet you and Dad had a huge reception and went to Niagara Falls for your honeymoon."

Mother corrected this also. "You can't go to Niagara Falls when you only have one day off. Vinson and I came back to our rented apartment. Aunt Iola and Uncle Hubert, while Vinson and I were in Kentucky, drove Mr. Leonard's pick-up truck to Pugh's Wholesale and got the furniture which your Dad and I bought.

"Iola and Hubert placed all the furniture by the time Vinson and I got home. It couldn't have been more perfect."

"Then you arranged that, too."

"Well, of course, Patricia," Mother answered and resumed peeling.

"Just one more question, Mother, how about the huge reception?"

"I don't call four people a huge crowd. Iola had prepared fried chicken, mashed potatoes and her wonderful biscuits with her homemade blackberry jelly. She picked the blackberries on Cow Creek."

That was the last straw. "How ordinary. Your wedding wasn't anything like *Father of the Bride*."

Mother stopped peeling, rested her palms on the edge of the table and looked straight at me. "Wake up, Patricia. This was real life, not Hollywood!"

Looking at the marble-sized potatoes, I agreed.

Nadine and Vinson on their first date

THE MASCOT

Hearing a car door slam, I ran to look out the front window to see if it was Mother coming home. She had gone to Jackson's Mill with the Busy Bee Homemakers' Club to attend their annual conference where there were to be nationally recognized speakers conducting workshops on the art of homemaking. Only the hope of radical improvement in this area had persuaded Dad to fork over the ten dollars to cover the cost of the conference.

Opening the door, I heard Mother's laughter as she and her friends briefly relived the funny happenings at the meeting. I saw Geebe Jones, the chauffeur of the group, getting Mother's luggage from the car trunk, and Mother trying to pull something through the car window. Whatever the object was, it was too large to come through the window of the car. This approach not working, Mother opened the car door and jerked the thing out.

Geebe carried Mother's luggage to the front door, and the two waved good-bye, commenting again on how worthwhile the conference had been. Mother, unable to get her arms around the thing, picked it up by an opening which appeared to be at its top. She managed, with my holding the screen door wide open, to carry it into the living room.

Under better lighting and upon close scrutiny, I saw the thing had all the features of a decapitated human body with the arms and legs severed from its trunk. The proportions, along with curves and bulges, qualified it for an exact replica of my mother's size 18 1/2 nude body.

"See what I made," Mother said with uninhibited pride.

"I certainly do!" I answered, trying not to reveal my uncertainty about exactly what it was.

"It was the best one at the conference."

"I'm sure it was," I said, hoping that sometime in the not too distant future the thing's identity would be made known, without my having to come right out and ask.

"It will come in real handy," she said.

"No house should be without one," I answered.

"I don't know how I've made it all these years without it."

"Me either," I said, hoping curiosity did not show in my voice.

"When I'm making myself a dress, I can just fit it on this dress form and come up with an exact fit."

Relieved that the thing had been identified, the next question for me was how it had come into being. Unwilling to play games anymore, I just asked. "How did you make it so exact, with the right curves and all?"

"The experts at the conference showed us how to do all kinds of valuable and necessary things." Bubbling over with enthusiasm, Mother continued, "Some of the conference leaders had their Ph.D.'s in home economics. Do you know that the doctor who showed us how to do these dress forms had just finished writing her dissertation on this very subject?"

It was evident that Mother was impressed by all of these degrees. But as I looked the form up and down, I didn't think this was what Dad had in mind when he reluctantly gave up his ten dollars.

"You never said how you made it."

"Oh, yes, well, you have someone wrap your body from the shoulders down to your thighs with masking tape. Then they put a coat of shellac over the tape. Of course, you can't move until the shellac dries and the form hardens."

"What if you have an emergency? You know, like you need to go to the bathroom or something?"

"You just don't!" she answered firmly. "Your form would get all out of shape."

Checking out the form once again, I agreed that additional warping should be avoided at all cost. "You might end up with your belly button right between your boobs," I said without thinking. Mom couldn't keep a straight face at that thought.

"Once this thing—the form," I added quickly, "hardens, how do you get out of it?"

"Simple, just slit it down the rear and back out."

While trying to keep from laughing, just imagining Mother backing out of this thing bare butt first, a disturbing thought came to mind. I recalled that when I pulled a sticky Band-Aid off my arm, all the hair came off with it. I felt myself blushing at the thought of my Mother void of hair from her thighs up to her neck.

Not daring to be too direct in my next question, I asked, "But didn't pulling that tape off your bare skin hurt?"

"Don't be silly. We kept our underthings on, wrapped ourselves in cheese cloth and then put the tape on our bodies."

"Oh!" I said with a sigh of relief.

But there never seemed to be a place for "it." You can't just leave a thing like that sitting in the livingroom to be viewed by impressionable young eyes. Even worse, what if the preacher paid a visit? It was too large to fit under the bed; it rolled over on one shoulder or another when you tried to disguise it as a waste paper basket; and somehow it just wasn't right as a lamp shade. So, it ended up in the attic.

One morning when I was getting ready for school, a gasp coming from Mother brought me quickly to her side. She stood pointing in horror at the open-bed garbage truck driving down the street. Mounted on a broomstick and stuck on top of the garbage truck, Mother's dress form could be seen silhouetted against the early morning sky. Her dress form had replaced the teddy bear which once held this proud position as the mascot for the city garbage truck.

"Your Dad cleaned the attic yesterday, didn't he?"

90

"Yes," I said softly, hoping not to be heard.

"I'll never be able to face my friends again. Everybody will know that's my nude body—I mean form."

"Yes," I said just above a whisper.

Mother cringed in shame and embarrassment every time she heard the rattling and roaring of the approaching and departing garbage truck.

As for my honest reaction on the subject, I was glad the form had finally found a useful place in society. What other girl could brag that her mother, or her form, that is, was a mascot for the city garbage truck?

THE CASE OF THE
MISSING COMBINATION

For a week, as soon as supper was finished and Mother began washing the dishes, Dad retreated to the basement. Soon we heard hammering and sawing.

Following seven days of my wondering what was being built, Dad proudly carried into the dining room a rectangular box with the woodwork yet unfinished.

"What is it?" I asked.

"A box," he answered.

"I can see that, but what's it for?"

No response.

Mother did not stop washing the dishes, nor enter into the conversation. She just listened, glancing into the dining room every once in a while from her post in the kitchen.

"It could serve as a small coffin," I suggested. As the words escaped my lips, I felt my throat tighten. The cat must have died, I thought. But no, I could see Miss Kitty lapping up her supper in the kitchen.

Dad, ignoring my statement about the coffin, situated the box underneath the window, making it clearly visible to anyone coming in the front door. A combination lock dangled from the front.

"Since things have a way of disappearing around this house, I've made a box to keep my important papers in. I am thinking it would be very difficult to misplace a box this size. It's too big to be put in the refrigerator's lettuce crisper. That was the fate of the alarm clock, you know," he said dryly.

Silence emanated from the kitchen. "The box doesn't exactly match the rest of the dining room furniture," I said.

"The aim is not to camouflage the box. I've decided high visibility is the key to hanging onto things around this house."

Mother must have opened the window because I thought I felt a cold draft coming from the kitchen.

Dad, not seeming to notice, continued, "I'm going to check each time I come in the front door to see if the box is still here. This should assure early detection of loss. I know from experience that the sooner I detect something is missing, the better chance I have of relocating it. Why, some things are lost so long around here that by the time I uncover them, they have become obsolete."

My female intuition alerted me to the fact that Dad had gone too far, so I did not venture any response to his last comments. For the ensuing weeks, I noticed my friends' viewing the box with questioning eyes but never daring to ask the obvious. As for Mother, she seemed to ignore the situation.

One day when I got home from school, Dad was waiting for me at the front door, trying to act casual when he was obviously rather excited. "I have a problem concerning the box," he announced.

"It's still there," I assured him.

"Yes, yes, I know that, but I can't get it open. I've lost the combination to the lock. I had it in my billfold and now it's gone."

"Didn't you memorize the combination?"

"Why should I memorize it when I wrote it down and put it in my billfold?" he asked impatiently.

The answer to the question was so obvious that I didn't dare give it.

"Now, would you ask your Mother what the combination is? I have to have some tax papers out of there tonight."

"Oh! You gave Mother a copy of the combination?"

"No, no, but she would have figured it out by now. Nadine wouldn't let a challenge like this pass her by."

"How would she figure out a combination?"

"Perhaps she sandpapered her finger tips sensitizing them to the tumblers inside the lock to determine the correct combination, or maybe she used a stethoscope to listen to the tumblers until she heard the right clicks. How should I know? Just please ask her!"

"Why don't you ask Mother? You two talk about everything else."

"We don't talk about the box."

Complying with Dad's request to extract the needed information from Mother, I volunteered to help her with the dishes that evening. Since that in itself raised her suspicion, I decided upon being direct and going straight to the heart of the issue.

"Mom, Dad has lost the combination to the box, and he wanted me to ask you for it."

Her eyes widened as she asked, "What box?"

"The one in the dining room." I answered, going along with her innocence.

"How would I know the combination?" she questioned, appearing to be aghast at such a thought.

Not daring to tell her about some of Dad's suggestions on how she might have acquired such information, I just shrugged my shoulders.

"Vinson never told me the combination!"

"Yes, I know," I agreed. "I just thought . . . "

"Well, I never. Here your Dad makes such a to do about things disappearing around here, builds a box to assure against loss of his important papers, and now he has lost the combination to the box which was to prevent the loss of his papers."

I couldn't disagree.

"Didn't he memorize the combination?"

"No."

I thought I caught a mischievous smile briefly cross her face.

"Well, well," she said.

"Mother, he is awfully concerned because there are some tax papers he has to have out of there tonight."

Mom shrugged as if to say what can I do? However, an hour later, as I walked through the dining room, I noticed the lock was unlocked.

No reference was ever made to this mysterious occurrence. But it was obvious that the lock was not functional anymore, and, indeed, it became lost. "The box" still remains as a reminder that Nadine once again rallied to a challenge.

FIRE

I was walking from a movie with friends when I looked skyward and saw a red glow rotating in slow even motions above 825 Saunders Street, my home address. What could the ominous light be! a UFO? an ambulance? a police car? a fire truck? or perhaps all four? I took off running.

As I turned the corner of Kanawha Terrace at Saunders, "Stop!" came a voice. "Where are you headed, girl?" demanded a policeman. "Can't you see the street has been blocked off?"

I backed away in silence. As soon as I rounded the corner where I could no longer be seen, I raced through the back yards of houses facing Saunders, looking carefully at the ground, so as not to trip. I looked skyward only momentarily to see if the circling red light was still visible. It was. Something was wrong at home. My stomach rotated in the same slow movements as the light above.

Making it to my own back yard, I tried to hush my gasps for breath, so I wouldn't be heard by who or whatever might be in the vicinity. I saw nothing. Flattening myself against the outside wall, I slowly and cautiously moved toward the front walk. I now heard static and sudden bursts of voices coming from what I decided must be two-way radios.

Once at the corner of the house, I made a break for the front sidewalk. I stopped abruptly. Between the house and me stood a solitary male figure.

Slowly moving my eyes from the ground up, I saw that he wore a pair of untied expensive dress shoes, without socks, cotton khaki work pants, and a well tailored fleece-lined sportscoat.

His hair was uncombed, and his eyes were expressionless. Smoke from his cigarette slowly encircled his head, evaporating into the red glow that surrounded us.

"What's wrong, Dad?" I asked.

"The house might be on fire," he answered in a matter of fact way, removing the cigarette from his mouth.

"What do you mean? The house might be on fire. Don't you know?"

"All I know is that your mother woke me out of a deep sleep screaming, 'Fire! Fire! The house is on fire!' I jumped up, got dressed, and ran out. Now you tell me . . . do you see any fire?"

"Where are Mother and David?"

"I guess they're still inside. I told Nadine that if she and David were coming out to bring the box. I had to get my new jacket and shoes."

The box, which I referred to earlier, was four feet long, a foot deep and wide, filled with smaller metal boxes containing Dad's "important papers" and dime collection.

"I think I'd better give them a hand," I said, moving in the direction of the house.

Dad was saying, as I stepped onto the front porch, "I hope if the house is on fire the firemen just let it burn. I work with a man whose house caught fire. The firemen did more damage with their hatchets—chopping up the windows, roof and walls—than did the fire. What they didn't chop up, they water-logged. I got fire insurance, but it doesn't cover vandalism."

His voice trailed off as I walked into the house. My entrance was unhampered since the firemen were concentrating on Hale's house next door.

Our house was dark and silent. I moved toward Mother and Dad's bedroom. My eyes slowly adjusted to the dark. From the bedroom doorway, I saw Mother sitting on the edge of the bed engrossed in the activity next door.

My voice, shattering the silence, startled even me. "What are you doing sitting here in bed when the house is on fire?"

"The house is not on fire," Mother answered, not moving her attention from the scene next door.

"Dad said you told him the house was on fire!"

"Well, I thought it was. I woke up, looked out the window, and saw these hooded men with hatchets going between our house and Hale's. What would you think?"

"It could have been the Ku Klux Klan," I suggested.

"The Ku Klux Klan wear white sheets and don't drive red fire engines," she said.

"How do you know our house is not on fire?"

"As soon as your dad left, and before I woke up David, I hollered out the window and asked the hooded ones what was happening."

"Well?"

"Well, they said somebody had reported a fire at Hale's, and they were investigating. The Hales are on vacation, you know."

"When are you going to let Dad know that our house isn't on fire?"

"Look! After I woke him up, somebody else is going to have to tell him, not me!"

Not until the activity next door subsided did Mother move. When she did, it was quick as a flash. She was out of the bed, bounding toward the dining room where the box was kept. With great gusto she pulled the box toward the front door.

In close proximity to her sudden burst of energy, I heard the front door open, footsteps, and then my dad's voice. "You been in here tugging on that box all that time, Nadine?"

"You told me if I was coming out to bring the box, Vinson."

"Well, if there had been a fire, the box would have been long gone by now!"

"What do you mean, if there had been a fire?" questioned Mother, managing to interject a great deal of inquisitiveness into her voice.

"I mean, Nadine, we can all go back to bed. Neither our house nor Hale's house is on fire." Dad clunked down the hallway muttering to himself, "Seems a body just can't get any rest around here."

"Ain't that the truth!" answered Mother, shaking her head in utter disgust.

"I would like to see Herb, please."

"Mr. Burgess is very busy today. Do you have an appointment?"

"No, just tell Herb that Nadine wants to see him."

"Nadine who?"

"The red-headed Nadine. He'll know. You see, when we were teenagers, my father moved back to St. Albans and organized a little orchestra, Miller's Melody Makers. Grace played the piano, Drusetta played first violin, I played second, Carl, my brother, played saxophone, and Herb played the trumpet."

"Madam, this is a business office," the secretary snapped.

At this moment, Mr. Burgess's office door was flung open and a hand appeared through the opening holding papers seemingly meant for the secretary.

"Herb is that you?" Nadine asked hesitantly.

A head that apparently went with the hand now extended beyond the door's edge. "Well, Nadine, I haven't seen you in years. Come on in."

"I was just telling your secretary about our orchestra," Mother chattered on as she entered his office.

The secretary ducked her head as if absorbed in reading.

"I'll never forget," said Herb; "that was quite an orchestra. By the time we got tuned up for our performance, the audience had gone home. What are you up to nowadays, Nadine?"

"You know Carl owns a weekly newspaper, the *Putnam Democrat*, and he has taken me on as his sales representative for advertising."

Herb shook his head, "And you want me to buy an ad. Certainly, just work out the details with my secretary. I'd like to have the ad in this week's paper."

Nadine agreed, made the arrangements with the now not so reluctant secretary, and went home to call Carl. "Carl I've sold a full page ad to Herb Burgess."

"That's wonderful. I've never had an advertising representative even get past Herb's secretary. Just leave it to you. When is the ad to be in?"

"This week's paper, Carl."

"Nadine, this week's paper just went to press. I explained the deadline to you."

"Stop the press!"

"No, Nadine, you just have to learn that in the newspaper business a deadline is a deadline."

"Then run it next week."

As I stood in the hall, eavesdropping was unavoidable since men talk so loudly. When Mother hung up, I reached for the receiver, but she held her hand up saying, "Patty, hold your call. I just thought of another sales prospect." She dialed the number and started the sale.

"Tom, this is Nadine. How is your funeral business doing?"

"Can't complain. People dying everyday."

"I understand all the bodies you put in caskets aren't dead," Mother teased.

A chuckle was heard on the other end of the line, "You must be talking about that joke we played on old Squeakie Jones. He ain't too bright, you know."

"I hear Ted Means was involved," Mother said.

"Yep, it was Ted who got in a casket and played dead. When Squeakie came in, I asked him to watch the corpse while I went to get a bite to eat. Then I hid behind the curtain to watch. Ted Means started slowly rising from the casket making all these groaning sounds. Before I knew what had

101

happened, Squeakie, his eyes about to pop out, screamed, 'Lay down you S.O.B! You're supposed to be dead!' He yanked a flashlight from his hip pocket and cracked Ted right between the eyes. Squeakie ran, and Ted had to have three stitches."

Mom laughed and then went to work, "Well, Tom, I was just calling to see if you wanted to place another ad."

"If you can get it in this week's paper. I'm running a special on prearranged funerals."

"We'll get to it," was Mother's response.

Immediately she phoned Carl, "Tom bought an ad for the funeral home. It has to get in this week because they're running a special on prearranged funerals."

"Nadine, I told you that this week's paper is already off the press and in the mail room. If you don't start paying attention to deadlines, you're going to need to purchase a prearranged funeral. If the customers don't get you, I'm going to."

My uncle would complain to me, "Your Mother can sell anything, but when it comes to timing she is always off. I've explained about deadlines to Nadine. It seems not to make any impression, or she chooses to ignore it."

I knew, but never said, that Mother refused to be restricted by the confines of time in any situation, not just the newspaper deadline.

THE BEAT GENERATION

Age sixteen introduced many firsts into my life. I had my first real job, working as a cashier in a supermarket. That Christmas was the first time I ever had any money to speak of to buy gifts, and the first store-bought gift for my younger brother, David, had to be special. After much shopping, I settled on a toy drum set with drums, cymbals and a foot pedal.

It has never been decided if by this purchase I helped awaken David's dormant musical talent or if I opened Pandora's Box. Initially I am sure it was the latter. Mother would roll her eyes at me as the thumping, bumping, ringing sounds created by David on his drums reverberated throughout our house. Dad would come stumbling down the stairs at 5:00 p.m., looking all strung out with nerves on razor edge as a result of his futile attempt to get a day's sleep after working the midnight shift.

Finally the drum set disappeared. Nobody seemed to know its fate. However, David still had the drum sticks and his unquenchable thirst to beat on something—anything: tin cans and pans and/or cow bells and jar lids suspended like mobiles from the ceiling.

Mother, in self-defense, not having money for another drum set, acquired (somewhere-somehow) oil drums in a variety of sizes and shapes which gave off different tones. Too unsightly for the living room, they were relegated to the basement.

This seemed to solve many problems. David could thump and beat, with a floor between the drums and Dad. Dad could sleep.

With Dad and David occupied, Mother had time to unleash her creativity. However, for me, this arrangement proved irritating when I had friends over and those rumbling sounds erupted from below.

But then nothing stays the same, and as David got older, rock-n-roll bands took his fancy. In the sixties, these teenage bands were not in short supply. Neither training nor talent was required to be a member, just the possession of an instrument.

Since oil drums did not qualify as a rock-n-roll instrument, David began his unrelenting campaign for a set of drums. Perhaps the request did not fall on deaf ears, but it most certainly fell on an empty billfold.

These bands had a problem other than finding members who owned instruments—the problem of finding a place to practice. Neighbors would only tolerate so much noise before calling the police.

David's friend Paul managed a band which had been warned on several occasions concerning its contribution to noise pollution. So Paul was scouting for a new place to practice. Preying on David's weakness for rock-n-roll, Paul made our house his target. Paul's line of persuasion was, "Erwin, if you can't be in a band, the second best thing would be to let a band practice at your house. When the drums are not in use, maybe you could practice."

This made sense to David who reasoned if Mom and Dad could only see how talented he was, they would buy him a set of drums. Paul's aim had been to gain the use of our house by persuading David, who in turn had to persuade Mother without the knowledge of Dad.

Mother's question was, "Where is Vinson going to be while all this is going on?"

"At work," David answered.

Mother's second question was, "Do you know any of the band members?"

"No, Mom, but they're okay. They're Paul's friends." Seeing that Mother was not yet convinced, David continued, "You always say, 'Birds of a feather flock together.' "

A frown of concern crept across Mom's forehead. But since there was not an emphatic *no*, the green light was given by David to Paul for the next Saturday, when Dad would be working. Paul in turn activated the plan.

Paul's arrival at the appointed hour for practice, 1:00 p.m., was announced by a loud rap at our door. David, who had been anxiously waiting, was the official greeter. "Where is the band? Aren't they coming?"

"Take it easy, Erwin; you'll find creative people like my band members aren't confined to time like we are. They just come when they come."

"Well, they had better come and go before my Dad gets here at 5:00 p.m."

"I'm in charge, and everything is under control," Paul assured. "While we're waiting, we can start moving the furniture."

"Move furniture?" echoed David. "You didn't say anything about moving furniture before, Paul."

"Well, sure, we have to make room for the amplifiers near the electrical outlets. Just set those lamps on the dining room table." Paul decided. "Now, let's see. The two of us can move the TV to make room for the electric guitar, and we can just set those tables and that rocking chair on the porch to make room for the bass drums and saxophone players.

"Oh, yeah, we'll set the coffee table on top of the dining room table, so the three singers can stand here in the middle of the room. Let's get busy, Erwin. No time to waste."

David reluctantly joined Paul. Just as they finished rearranging the furniture, an old dented car pulled up. Out climbed a man carrying a saxophone and wearing a tee shirt which hit him at his belly button, leaving the rest of his beer belly exposed above faded jeans.

"That must be one of the kid's dads, but where is his kid?" David turned and looked at Paul.

"No, that's Alphonso. He plays the sax."

"But that's not a kid. That's a grown man, and I do mean grown," David protested.

"What do you mean, kid? I don't have kids in my band. This isn't any teeny bopper band. This is a big time band, Man."

"Oh my gosh, Paul, do they all look like him? He looks like he hasn't shaved or combed his hair in a week."

"I told you, Erwin, these are creative artists. They don't get hung up on the physical, time, and all that." Paul gave David a little shove as he made his way to the door. "This is the place, Alphonso. Step right in."

Alphanso said not a word. Just a faint grunt was audible, as he swaggered into the house eyeing everything. He was soon followed by the other band members, who weren't very talkative either. When they did say something, Paul took the role of interpreter. However, most communication was done through eye contact, body language, quick snaps of the fingers, and those barely audible grunts.

David was simply awed by all the equipment, especially the drums, and forgot appearances, time, and place.

It was when the huge amplifiers were plugged in, causing the lights to dim, and the band started tuning up that Mother came from wherever it was that she went when these kinds of things were happening. However, it was too late. The band was in control as they ripped into their first number, and the three singers gave relief to the now sagging sofa as they stood to blare out, "Leroy Brown's back in town . . . ."

Within a few minutes, the neighborhood kids crowded in. Those unable to squeeze into the living and dining rooms clung to the screendoor like flies. Hands clapped, bodies swayed, and time stopped.

Nobody noticed a 1952 green Chevrolet circle the block several times and finally park a block away because the spaces in front of the Erwin house were taken. Nor did anyone pay any attention to a man clad in khaki work clothes and safety-toed shoes carrying a lunch box enter the front yard. This man lit up a cigarette and slowly inhaled as he watched with curiosity the scene in front of him—a front porch packed with furniture and writhing human bodies, the roof pulsating to a jungle beat, and the inside lights giving off the flicker of a neon light due to the electrical overload of the amplifiers. Seeing the futility of trying to enter the house by the front door, the man circled to the back door and entered.

Nadine, standing in the dining room a movin' and a groovin', was startled by a loud, "Psst," and a familiar voice saying, "Nadine," followed by, "What the hell's going on in my house?"

"Vinson, is that you?"

"Strange as it may seem, Nadine, it is."

"And it must be five?"

"That's right, Nadine."

"I haven't even started your supper."

"Nadine, who are these people? Have you leased our living room out to the county jail, a half-way house, or what?"

"Oh, no, that's little Paul Maxwell and his little band. David is letting them practice here."

"Nadine, you must have been looking through the wrong end of your binoculars to think there is anyone little in there," Dad gave a nod toward the living room. "That two-hundred-pounder looks like he just escaped Sing Sing."

"No, Vinson, he's on parole."

Dad, narrowing his eyes at her reply, directed, "Get them out of here, Nadine."

Mother, standing on her tip toes trying to stretch her 5'2" height into 5'3", cleared her voice and yelled, "Boys, Mr. Erwin is home, and you'll have to go!"

Nothing happened. I doubt if she even heard herself over the racket.

She turned and looked at Dad whose eyes were still narrowed and who now tapped his index finger impatiently on

107

the table piled on top of the dining table. She then turned and surveyed the band again. Shrugging her shoulders, she hastened down the basement steps.

Following one last loud ping of the electric guitar, the electricity went off—dead silence. The silence was broken by Mother's voice explaining that there was a power outage.

This was followed by those barely audible grunts and the non-verbal communication that the band used when setting up. Only they now came in reverse order as the equipment was dismantled. The band left, followed by its groupies.

Mother, having waved good-bye to the last departing car, started toward the kitchen and announced supper would be started just as soon as she put the fuses back in the fuse box. This seemed to pacify Dad, and David lapsed into hatching his next plan.

A BIRDCAGE
IS A BIRDCAGE IS A BIRDCAGE

Mother was helping my Aunt and Uncle move from Winfield, a neighboring town ten miles away, to our hometown of St. Albans. The previous owner of the house that Carl and Mary bought just upped and moved without cleaning the garage. When my uncle asked him what to do with the stuff, the man said, "Keep what you want and throw away the rest."

Mother, being one who called upon old adages whenever they fit her purpose, chose "Waste not want not" for this occasion. She was right there on the scene to see that nothing of value was tossed.

Picking her way through empty and half-empty paint cans, she swept aside cobwebs with her outstretched hands as her eyes slowly adjusted to the dark garage. Back among the shadows of the farthest corner, she spied a birdcage. Something in her mind clicked! "Look, Carl, here is an extra fine *deluxe* birdcage—almost like new. Do you need the cage?"

"Nope, don't have a bird, don't want a bird," Uncle Carl answered.

"I sure would like to have that cage!" Mother coaxed.

"Nadine, you don't have anything to put in it, do you?"

"No, I just need the cage."

Uncle Carl, having full knowledge of Mother's unique human behavior (which I have on occasion heard him label as, "Down right *BEEZAR!*"), said, "Take the cage, Nadine."

That evening he packed Mother and me along with the birdcage into his car and took us home. Mother insisted on holding the cage on her lap, so the glass feeder wouldn't get broken. As soon as the car pulled up to the curb, Mother threw the car door open, jumped out, walked over to our next door neighbor's and carefully placed the cage on their porch directly in front of the door.

109

When she returned to the car to get her purse, Carl, with a stunned look on his face, asked, "Nadine, why are you setting the cage over there? Don't you want it?"

"No, I don't want it. I'm returning the birdcage to Mrs. Hale."

"How could you 'return' a birdcage, which could obviously never have been Mrs. Hale's, since you found it in my garage?"

"Carl, I borrowed her birdcage to keep David's hamster in. I'm using this one you gave me to replace that one."

"What happened to the first cage, Nadine?"

"It's gone."

"Where is the hamster?"

"It's gone."

"Nadine, I won't ask where the cage and hamster vanished to because your answer will be so vague that we might as well not go into it. But how long has the cage been gone?"

Mother, after some calculating on her fingers, answered, "Five years."

"Now, let me get this story straight, for it's a goody. You borrowed the lady's birdcage, and five years later you place another cage on her front porch without even knocking on her door to offer an explanation."

Mother shook her head in agreement. "That's what I've done, taken her birdcage back."

My Uncle, trying to puzzle this out in his mind, continued, "I wonder if the lady recalls lending you a birdcage five years ago, and what will her reaction be when she comes out her door in the morning to find this cage?"

Mother, nodding her head up and down, said, "She knows I got it."

"Has anything been said about this in the last five years.?"

"No." For the first time Mother shook her head in the negative, "Nobody has mentioned it. When I saw the birdcage in your garage, I just remembered." Her head nodded in the affirmative again.

Uncle Carl, realizing that was all he was going to learn, drove off.

As soon as I awoke the next morning, I stationed myself at my window to see what Mrs. Hale's reaction to the unexplained birdcage would be. After not too long a wait, I saw Mrs. Hale with curlers in her hair and still wearing her robe, poke her head out the front door. Leaning over to pick up her paper, she abruptly stopped halfway into her bend. She did a second take of the *deluxe* cage. Then she looked up the road, down the road, and toward heaven. Shrugging her shoulders, she retrieved both the paper and birdcage and went inside.

"Things must be hectic at your house nowadays?" said Mrs. Littlejohn, a neighbor lady.

I thought through the last few days. Everything seemed pretty much the same—quieter than usual in fact. "I hadn't noticed," I answered.

"Your mother's workdays are either getting started earlier or lasting later."

"What do you mean?"

"Well, I was awakened this morning at about two o'clock by the sound of running water. I thought a water pipe broke under the house, or somebody turned the fire hydrant on. Since I could check the hydrant by simply looking out my front window, I decided to eliminate that possibility first." Mrs. Littlejohn started laughing.

I waited for her to finish. "Well" I said, "What's so funny?" She just kept laughing.

"What did you see?"

Finally gaining control of herself she said, "I saw your mother."

"You've been seeing her for over a decade."

"Yes, but I never saw her watering the lawn at 2:00 a.m. before. You'll have to admit that would not be when most people water their lawns."

Mrs. Littlejohn was beginning to make me feel a bit uncomfortable. "How do you know it was Mother?"

Mrs. Littlejohn started laughing again. "Because she had your little brother's big silver five-pronged marshall's badge to clasp her buttonless robe together. Now, who else could it be but Nadine?"

I shrugged my shoulders.

Mrs. Littlejohn went on, "I pecked on the window to get her attention and even waved. I was checking to see if she was sleep walking."

Thinking and hoping this might be the explanation, I asked anxiously, "And what did Mother do?"

"She just waved back and continued watering the lawn, as if it were six o'clock in the evening. You know, like it was the normal thing to be doing."

"Well, of course it's the normal thing to do," I said; "You have to wait until it cools down to water, so you don't wilt your grass. Everybody knows that."

"Oh," she said pondering my explanation. A few seconds passed, and she began nodding her head up and down in agreement.

I felt very pleased with myself. Until it dawned on me that Mother's antics were beginning to seem logical. Not only that, but I could make them seem logical to others.

To get my thinking straight, I asked Mother about the incident. "Mother, were you watering the lawn at two this morning?"

"I think it was about that time," she answered.

"Why?" I asked.

"Why what?"

"Why at two in the morning?"

"I couldn't sleep, and it was the only thing I could think of to do. Is there anything wrong with that?" she asked.

"Not at all," I said with a sigh of relief because our explanations didn't match.

The rabbit sat nibbling a piece of lettuce, uninhibited by the three pairs of eyes peering at it or by its high visibility as it sat in a cage in the middle of Evans Super Market.

"Oh, Vinson, when I was little I always wanted a white rabbit with pink eyes. Its fur looks so soft."

Dad, a lover of animals, when they were kept in their proper place—outside the house, was engrossed in observing the animal and did not answer Mother.

"Can I hold it? Can I? I'd love this bunny for Easter," David said with the enthusiasm and excitement that only a child is free enough to show.

"I'll ask this clerk coming down the aisle," Mother volunteered.

The six eyes shifted to the handsome young man with the crop of curly hair and broad smile that lit up his hazel eyes. "Mister, Mister, over here." Mother was waving her hands in the air to gain the clerk's attention.

"Nadine, would you stop! Everybody in the store is looking at us."

Mother, ignoring Dad's directive, gave a leap which cleared the floor by at least three inches, while simultaneously waving her arms. "Yoo hoo, we're here by the rabbit cage."

"Hush up, Nadine, or they're going to take the rabbit out of the cage and put you in it."

"Then I could hold the bunny!" said David, jumping up and down clapping his hands.

The young man of about twenty or so could not ignore these three who focused their full attention on him, even if he wanted to. His face flushed from all of the attention, he walked over quickly and asked, "May I help you?"

David, pointing into the cage, pleaded, "Can I hold that bunny?"

wanted to. His face flushed from all of the attention, he walked over quickly and asked, "May I help you?"

David, pointing into the cage, pleaded, "Can I hold that bunny?"

"Afraid not," answered the clerk. "It might bite, the store would be liable, and besides, it's on loan for our Easter display of egg dye and Easter candy."

While David eyed the bright jelly beans and chocolate Easter eggs, Mother took up the conversation. "Maybe whoever lent the store this bunny would sell us one. Could you give me the owner's name?"

"Yes, Ma'am, I'll get it from the office." The clerk, looking relieved that he had quelled the commotion so simply, disappeared into the office and reappeared quickly, information in hand. He gave it to Mother who in turn passed it to Dad.

"You've been so helpful, and, by the way, what's your name?"

"Doug Call; if I can be of any more help, just let me know," he said ready to make a fast exit. But Mother chattered on.

"Coll, Coll, there are some Colls out at Tornado. You related to them?"

"No, we cash their checks though. They spell their name with an *o*, and we spell ours with an *a*."

Mother was confident that with more interrogation she would uncover some of Doug's relatives that she knew. She was poised for the next set of questions, when Dad nudged her saying, "Come on, Nadine. This boy has work to do."

"Speaking of work," Mother continued with pride now showing in her voice, "I bet you know our daughter. She works here as a cashier after school, Patty Erwin, the little blonde. This is her dad, Vinson, and David, her brother."

Doug swallowed hard as his eyes widened with surprise, for he had been planning on asking Patty for a date.

"Oh, yes, I know Patty." He cleared his throat and looked down.

"Her name is Patricia!" my Dad said emphatically.

Mother, turning in Dad's direction, added, "But, she likes to be called Patty."

Doug, seeing an opportunity to leave, took off. However, he had not seen the last of the Erwins, for this was not to be a brief passing encounter between a clerk and customers, but an encounter that would evolve into a lifelong commitment.

David got his white Easter Bunny, but not without incident. It seemed the breeder of the rabbits lived on a dirt road that with the spring rains was nearly impassable. After the purchase and getting Nadine, David and the rabbit calmed down and into the car, Dad put the car in reverse to turn around. The tires spun. He shifted into high and then into reverse trying a rocking motion to gain traction, but the tires were sucked deeper and deeper into the mud.

"Vinson, call Phillip's wrecker service."

"Last time you got us in a similar mess, Nadine, your cousin charged me an arm and a leg. You must be in cahoots."

Mother pressed her lips together and did not answer.

"Slide over here, Nadine. When I signal, put the car in reverse and slowly, slowly let the clutch out. I'll drop rocks in front of the rear tires. Then you put it into low. Are you listening, Nadine?"

Mother nodded yes.

Dad had just gotten the rocks and walked up behind the car, when Mother, thinking she heard the signal, put the car in reverse and popped the clutch.

Dad yelled, "No, Nadine."

Thinking he said, "Go, Nadine," she put the car in low gear and popped the clutch again.

In close succession came David's screaming giggles and exclamation, "Look, I got a chocolate-covered Daddy!"

116

curly haired clerk at Evans' flashed into Dad's mind. No, it was that boy who steered them up this mud-slick road!

This fact did not place Doug in Dad's good graces. However, Doug slowly won Dad's favor by helping him decipher Mother's grocery lists (which Dad described as being written in hieroglyphics) when Dad shopped at Evans.

Finally, Doug started coming to the house. If he came when we were eating, Mother would give out her usual invitation, "Pull up a chair. We have plenty, and there's more on the stove. Don't be bashful."

Dad would eat with relish until Doug stopped. At which time Dad would say, "What's wrong? Don't you like the food?"

"Yes, sir, everything is delicious," Doug would reply with embarrassment.

"Here then, have more." Dad insisted, spooning more fried potatoes onto Doug's plate.

Even though Doug and Dad broke bread together, Dad was not ready for what was to follow.

"You mean Doug's coming here—at seven this evening—to ask your Dad?" Mother's voice showed both concern and disbelief as it got higher and higher with each statement, punctuating the question by cupping her hand over her mouth.

"Yes, we don't want to go behind your backs," I said, wishing this conversation never had to take place. I knew I was disappointing my parents, and I tried so hard not to disappoint anybody, especially my parents.

Mother's next comment confirmed what I already knew. "Your Dad and I wanted you to have more than a high school education."

"I'll go to college. I promise."

"Um," replied Mother as she looked down at the napkin she folded and unfolded repeatedly. Then she looked up with a smile and said, "Well, I'll just have to get busy

"I'll go to college. I promise."

"Um," replied Mother as she looked down at the napkin she folded and unfolded repeatedly. Then she looked up with a smile and said, "Well, I'll just have to get busy making your wedding dress; French *peau de soie* will be a nice fabric."

With a sigh of relief came, "Yes." I knew I could always depend on Momma's support.

Mother, then biting her lower lip and releasing it said, "I don't know how your Dad is going to take this. Doug is a wonderful person, but I don't think your Dad ever accepted the fact that someday you would marry, especially so young. Vinson and I were thirty-one years old when we married."

"Well, Doug says he wants to have a man-to-man talk with Dad."

"That suits me just fine. I plan to be long gone, and you should be too, Patty."

At seven Dad was sitting on the sofa, shoeless, smoking a cigarette, looking over the newspaper, and no doubt very conscious of the quiet which was foreign to our house. Hearing a voom-voom-voom given off by twin glass-packed mufflers, he looked over the top of his paper. Through the screen door he saw a fire engine red car, a 1957 sports model Chevy with a white top, fender skirts, whitewall tires, and continental kit, being parked.

Doug walked up on the porch. He was engrossed in practicing his speech, which he had changed several times, and nearly jumped out of his shoes when Dad's voice boomed, "Come on in. Door's open."

The hinges on the door squeaked as it was slowly opened and shut. Doug stood in the living room eyeball to eyeball with Vinson.

"Those hinges need to be greased," was Dad's greeting. With all this quiet, he welcomed company. As in fact, he usually did. "Sit down." Dad nodded toward the rocking chair.

Doug without hesitation obliged. His mouth was dry to the point his throat felt swollen; tension mounted

Looking at this man whom he had grown to respect, he realized that Dad had no idea of what this visit was about.

Dad, always anxious to talk politics, pointed to the front page of the paper, "If we leave it to the Republicans, they are going to get us smack into another depression. You are a Democrat, aren't you?"

"Yes, Sir," Doug answered quickly, knowing this would be a definite plus.

Then came silence as Dad took a drag from his cigarette in preparing to describe in vivid detail the "Republican debauchery of the Great Depression which crushed the hopes of so many 'little people.' "

Doug, fearing the loss of his voice if he did not get into his speech, broke the silence, "Mr. Erwin, you know Patty and I've been seeing a lot of each other. I mean, ah, well, we love each other and want to get married." The last sentence was spoken so hastily that Doug was not sure if it were intelligible.

There was no response—silence. Then Doug saw Dad's eyes narrow either to keep the cigarette smoke out or to reveal a pensive mood. Not another muscle moved—silence. Breathing deeply, Dad asked, "How much do you make as assistant manager of that store?"

"I'm expecting a raise but right now $4,600." Doug, seeing no reaction, interpreted this as a minus.

"You save any?" was the next question.

"Yes. I have a bank account, and I don't owe anybody anything; I mean money." Doug hoped this would end the questioning.

"Not even on that fancy car there?" Dad said nodding toward the Chevy.

"Just finished paying it off this month, sir."

Then came the awful heavy silence again. Doug managed to focus his eyes above Dad's on the cigarette smoke which curled upward in a counter clockwise movement. After several minutes, it occurred to Doug that the trial was over. A "no" or silence was the only answer he could have expected, for this man would never be able to say, "Yes, I'll give you my daughter." He would eventually take a secondary role in her life, but he would always feel a responsibility. Hadn't she been Nadine's and his first born? When God gives you a responsibility, you don't pass it off to somebody else. Sensitive to what might be going on in Vinson's mind, Doug excused himself from this meeting which had no formal closure.

When I came home, Dad and I did not have a long father/daughter talk. He simply said, "I understand you and Doug want to get married."

I answered emphatically, "Yes." All the while I was gripped by anxiety at knowing I was disappointing my parents. I did not have to search Dad's face to know there was concern.

But these uneasy feelings dissolved somewhat when Doug laughingly reported that a big white rolling pin had been sent to him by Mother with the attached note, "Keep Patty in line."

Symbolically, this was acceptance. Plans for the wedding were set in motion and culminated on October 11, 1959. As might have been expected, Mother was sewing the last seed pearl bead onto my wedding dress as I walked out of the house headed for the church.

"Mother, I've never seen a wooden Hula-Hoop before. Where did you get it?"

Mother held the large wooden hoop up, turning it this way and that. "It's not meant to be a Hula-Hoop, but I guess it could be used for that purpose, now that you mention it."

Dad was seated in the easy chair reading the paper. I plopped down on the sofa beside Mother to watch her put some finishing touches on her sketch of the beagle with sad eyes.

"That's really good, Momma."

She nodded her head in agreement. "Do you know whose dog this is?"

"No."

She was disappointed. "It's a picture of President Johnson's beagle." She looked me square in the face to see if that brought any sign of recognition. Seeing none, Mother went on, "You know, the dog that got all that news coverage because Johnson picked it up by its ears?"

Dad dropped the paper just enough to peep over the top. "Nadine, I'll never understand why the news media or you pick such obscure things to talk about and draw pictures of."

"Well, I think the media was unkind to pick on the President like that. Anybody who has been around dogs knows that's how you pick up pups. That's why God gave them long ears—to be used as handles, so to speak."

Dad shook his head in disbelief.

Mother pressed her lips tightly together momentarily and then continued, "I'm going to hook the President a rug using this sketch as my pattern. That Hoola-Hoop, as you call it, is what I'm going to use for hooking."

"Your Mother is our resident hooker," Dad chuckled.

"Vinson, watch your language."

"Mother, you mean that you are actually going to hook a picture of a beagle and send it to the President of the United States?"

"Well, he is human, too. He needs to know people care!"

Mother returned from the post office the day she mailed her creation to Johnson, expressing disbelief that public servants could be so rude. "It's a good thing I hooked the beagle instead of doing it in ceramics. It would have been broken into a million tiny pieces the way that postal clerk banged it around. I don't know what this country is coming to. Even a government worker doesn't show any respect. Here is a package addressed to the Honorable Lyndon Baynes Johnson, President of the United States of America, The White House, 1 Pennsylvania Ave., Washington, D.C., and the postal clerk is treating it like that, banging it around."

"How awful, Momma," I managed to interject, trying to maintain a sympathetic note in my voice.

She huffed on, "I'll have to admit that when I first placed the package on the counter the clerk was mighty careful about handling it."

"When I looked down in my purse, to hunt some change for postage, and looked back up, I caught this clerk holding the package up to his ear. I think he was listening for a timer. If he had tried to frisk me, he would have had his hands full. I'll tell you that! He even had the nerve to ask me what was in the package."

"Well, Momma, the package did not look like one of your run of the mill packages."

"What do you mean? The package was all done up in brown wrapping paper."

I tried to explain what I meant. "Yes, but the paper was held together with yarn and last year's Easter seals."

"That's simply all I had, and it worked fine. Everybody wants to be so conventional."

Mom's mailing the hooked beagle over five hundred miles away to Washington, D.C. did not end its influence on our lives. Every time Johnson had a televised news conference, Mother was right in front of the TV. She tried to recruit anybody else she could to join her. It wasn't that she had a sudden interest in economic, foreign, or domestic affairs; nor was she trying to cultivate such an interest in others. She directed us to scan the room in which the conference was being held in search of the hooked beagle.

Even when Johnson announced the national pride in some act of valor on the part of an individual, gloom prevailed in our house because at the end of the conference the beagle had not been sighted.

Mother was in her seventies when the Lyndon B. Johnson Memorial Library was opened. She always wanted to visit it to see if her beagle was on display.

"I'll never know if the President received my gift or not," she would worry. "You know when I wrote President Eisenhower a letter to tell him that I named your brother, David, after him, the President answered saying how honored he was to have a namesake."

"Mother, I named David myself, and I certainly didn't name him after Dwight David Eisenhower!"

"I know that, Patty. But it made the President feel good. In appreciation, he sent the letter plus an autographed picture of himself. I couldn't show the letter and picture to your dad, though."

"Why not?"

"He was such a staunch Democrat that I had to sneak the Hoover sweeper out to sweep the floor. He wouldn't have approved of my communicating in a positive way with a Republican president."

"Boom, boom, ain't it great to be crazy
Boom, boom, ain't it great to be crazy
Crazy and foolish all day long
Boom, boom, ain't it great to be crazy."

The voices of the youth department rang out as the bus bumped along, heading for a state Baptist Fourth-of-July retreat. Mother, singing along, directed with exaggerated hand movements; "Way down south where bananas grow, an ant stepped on an elephant's toe . . . ."

The girls of her Sunday school class who came on the retreat eagerly joined their comrade and teacher. Dora Lee, having twice refused promotions from Mother's class, was the oldest. Then there were Bernice, Tootsie and Marion.

Upon the bus's arrival at the campground, Mother went directly to the cafeteria and asked the cooks to pack brown bag lunches for her girls to take on their Saturday hike. In each lunch, she placed an American flag as a favor to commemorate the nation's birthday.

It was noon when the class hiked to a creek which meandered through a cow pasture. The timing was right, and Mother, pleased with the pastoral setting, told the girls that this was where they would have lunch. She then proceeded to pass out the sack lunches. "Oh, look what I have in my bag!" exclaimed Marion, "an American flag!" Marion held the flag up with great pride.

"I have one too!" beamed Bernice.

"You each got one," answered Mother.

Marion slowly turned the flag between her index finger and thumb, watching the flag gently move with the soft breeze and said, "This is the first American flag I ever had of my very own."

"You must treat it with respect," instructed Mother.

"Oh, I will. I'll find a special place to put it," promised Marion.

Following lunch, Mother pulled out her worn Bible storybook and read the story of the hospitality that Jesus found in the home of Mary and Martha. The story told how Mary bathed Jesus' dusty feet in expensive ointment and dried them with her own hair. Mother finished by saying, "This is a story of unselfishness and love. Can you imagine anyone drying someone's feet with her own hair?"

Bernice quickly answered, "I don't dry my baby brother's feet with my hair, but I'm always kissing his feet, and they got pee all over them."

"Well, Bernice, that would certainly take love," Mother managed to answer over the other's giggles. "Okay, now girls," Mother continued, "It's getting late. We'll have to take the shortcut across the cow pasture back to camp." The girls took off running, leaving Mother to bring up the rear.

Shortly Tootsie ran back, "Oh, Mrs. Erwin, you'll never believe where Marion put her American flag. Come quick!"

Mother speeded up her pace, and upon cresting a small knoll, she came upon this scene.

Marion stood holding a rock with her heels planted firmly, daring anyone to come near her sacred spot.

Dora Lee's raised voice chastised Marion, "You can't leave your flag there. It is disrespectful—as silly as running a pair of underwear up a flag pole."

"It's not," retorted Marion. "The flag is standing straight and pretty. See how it waves in the breeze."

"Take it down," Bernice demanded. "Do you want to hurt Mrs. Erwin's feelings?"

Marion, looking up, saw Mother and proudly moved aside, so Mother could have a clear view of the flag. The flag stood erect, having been secured in the biggest cow pile in the entire pasture. Mother watched the green flies buzz by in review, seeming to tilt their wings in a salute.

"Isn't that the dumbest thing you ever saw?" demanded Tootsie.

Marion's eyes sought out Mother's. "Did I do wrong, Mrs. Erwin?"

Mother glanced again at Old Glory standing erect on the pile. "Well, it isn't exactly Bunker Hill," she said wiggling her nose. The girls, including Marion, burst into hearty laughter, and Mother quickly added, "But, God knows your heart, Marion. Might be best, though, that we look for another spot."

"Yuck, I don't want to walk with Marion. She got cow poop on her flag," said Tootsie pushing ahead.

Mother handed Marion a napkin.

The next morning the girls were awakened by the camp bell announcing breakfast. The group, tired from their late night of pillow fighting and telling ghost stories, slowly emerged. Then, as it sometimes happens with youth, there was a surge of energy which permeated the room, having a positive effect on everyone but Mother. She turned back over and pulled the covers around her.

"Get up, Mrs. Erwin," called Dora Lee. "We're having pancakes and sausage for breakfast." The thought of food seemed to stimulate Mother slightly.

The girls ran out the door with jumps and giggles, leaving Mother behind. Mother got up as the last girl slammed the door behind her. She slipped into her clothes with the exception of her bra, which was missing. *I can't go braless to breakfast and opening exercises,* she thought. *Pastor Wolf would not approve.* She checked under stacks of pillows and clothes to no avail.

Smelling the pancakes and feeling the emptiness in her stomach, Mother decided the heck with Pastor Wolf. She flung the front door open and saw the flag pole in the center of the green. Waving in the breeze high atop the pole was not the flag, but Mother's 38C bra. The little group, standing wide-eyed and tense outside her door, then burst into smiles and began cheering as Mother with pride, flung back her shoulders, pushed out her chest and marched triumphantly to the mess hall.

"There's my girl," greeted Mom as I entered her front door, suitcase in hand. Following summer school exams, I was coming home for a visit.

Mom folded her warm soft arms around me in a hug then stepped back. Clapping her hands in a child-like manner, she said, "Guess what I made for you—a special treat." Before I could answer, with quick steps, she disappeared into the kitchen and returned with two cups of freshly brewed coffee. "We'll have a celebration, just the two of us."

Smelling the faint aroma of cinnamon and remembering that I mentioned in my last letter a yearning for rice pudding, I couldn't miss guessing, "Rice pudding!"

"How did you know? You're just getting so smart reading all those books."

I smiled and sipped my coffee, thinking that the Prodigal Son could not have received a warmer welcome than I did here.

Mother plopped a bowl of rice pudding filled with plump raisins warm from the oven in front of me. "I bet you've been curled up in that bathtub for days studying for those exams," she joked.

Doug and I lived in a one-room apartment in Marshall University's married student housing. Because Doug studied with the TV on, I sought refuge to study behind our only door, the one to the bathroom. Using sofa pillows to line the tub, I camped there.

"You know," Mother continued, "you are going to have curvature of the spine sitting all doubled up like that for four years. You'll probably be the shortest one in your graduating class."

"That's why I'm here, so I can stretch," I joked.

"Rice pudding good?"

"Yep, you want me to spit it out?" Seeing a puzzled look on her face, I explained. "You told me once if anything tasted good, spit it out immediately because it must be full of calories."

Remembering, Mother laughed and then said, "You will never guess who phoned me the other day."

I shook my head, no.

Leaning across the table, she looked me straight in the eyes, "Senator Byrd called me from Washington, D.C."

"Did he hear about your steaming open Doug's letters to me while he was in the army, a federal offense?" I kidded.

Mother waved her letter beneath my nose and said in a high excited voice, "See!"

The heading and signature revealed the letter was in fact from Senator Byrd. It read, "This letter confirms our conversation of May 14, 1965 . . . ."

"Okay, okay, so what did he call you about to begin with and why this letter of confirmation?"

"To be honest," said Mother, "I couldn't believe it was Bob either. You know how J.C. is always teasing when we talk."

J.C., hmmm, surely Mother wasn't referring to . . . .?

Picking up on my lapse into thought, Mother explained, "J.C. Reed, the lawyer. Anyway," she continued, "I kept saying, as the Senator tried to identify himself, 'Stop teasing, J.C., you devil you!' After the Senator explained his purpose for calling, he agreed to confirm our conversation with this letter."

"What was his purpose, Mother?"

"Bob asked how I felt the upcoming election would be going for him in this area," Mother answered casually.

"Why on earth would Bob ask you?"

Slightly offended by my words, Mother's mood shifted. "Some people see me as a political being," she replied, tilting her chin a bit. "Neighbors have even suggested that I run for

Councilwoman. I do work in all of the elections, and my brother does own the *Putnam Democrat Weekly News* for which I sell ads. Besides, I write the Senator."

"What do you write to the Senator about?" I asked, anxiously.

"My political concerns," she answered, flicking crumbs from the table.

Momentarily I was relieved, but then my mind flashed back to spring break when Marvin, from the next apartment, paid Doug and me a visit.

Marvin knew Doug went into a catatonic state while watching TV and that he spoke only during commercials. So as soon as the first commercial flashed on, Marvin quickly explained his visit. "You know, as a political science major, I am doing my internship in Congressman Ken Hechler's office."

Doug and I both nodded.

"Well," he continued, "I was going through Congressman Hechler's mail when I came across a letter from St. Albans. That is your hometown, isn't it?"

Doug and I nodded again.

"The letter was an inquiry about a loan for a Marshall student who had polio and needed financial assistance in order to continue school. It was sent by the mother."

I felt the heat of embarrassment creeping up my neck. This had a familiar ring.

"The student's name is Patricia, and the Mother's last name is Erwin. Wasn't that your maiden name?" he asked me.

I let the question hover in space while I studied my alternatives. If this had been a stranger making such an inquiry, and I'd had on a long-sleeved sweater instead of a short-sleeved one, I could have made one hand, perhaps two, disappear up the sleeves, thus appearing to have shriveled hands. Or, if I'd had on jeans instead of shorts, I could have made one foot, even two, disappear. No, that wouldn't work. If I concentrated real hard, maybe I could have made my face twitch. But since it was Marvin, who obviously knew that I had no such handicaps, I pretended to suffer from a momentary hearing loss to gain thinking time. "I didn't hear what you said, Marvin."

"The first part or the last?" he asked.

"Probably the last," I answered, nodding my head up and down.

Doug interceded in my behalf. "Marvin said, 'What a coincidence that there is another Marshall student from St. Albans whose name is Patricia and whose mother's name is Erwin.' The only difference being that she is a paraplegic, or something, which you, evidently, are not."

"I guess there could be another Patricia Erwin," agreed Marvin, squinting his eyes in a questioning manner.

"Yes, that's it," I said. "Every Tom, Dick and Harry in St. Albans is named Patricia Erwin."

"Tom, Dick, and Harry?" Marvin echoed.

"I mean, Erwin is a very common name back home, and there were at least fifteen Patricias in my class." At this, I started washing dishes, making as much racket as I could. This ploy always worked for Mother when she no longer wished to discuss a topic.

I heard Doug say, "Maybe someone is playing a hoax."

"Perhaps," Marvin said eyeing me suspiciously as he got up to leave.

The door had barely closed when I heard Doug let out a hoot. "Nadine is at it again," he said.

"I don't see anything to laugh about," I retorted. "Here I am forty miles away, and she embarrasses me through the mail." I felt like retreating to the tub forever.

"I've only been in the family for three years," said Doug, "and I've gotten used to Nadine. She probably knew we were short on tuition, and she didn't have any extra money to offer. You did have polio. That's no lie."

"Yes, when I was three!"

"So, she just got mixed up in her verb tense, or else she doctored the truth. I believe she calls that journalistic license. Besides, you didn't read the letter."

"But she wrote to our U.S. Congressman," I insisted.

"Nadine goes to high places," Doug answered.

"Speaking of high places, you didn't think it was so funny when she had our church praying for your broken clavicle."

"That was different," Doug objected. "If you remember, the way I found out about the prayer request was through reading the church newsletter which goes out to over a thousand people."

"But this was a U.S. Congressman," I protested.

Mother's flash of Senator Byrd's letter prompted me back into the present. I was tempted to remind Mother of this Marvin incident. But, I thought, why risk rekindling a worn issue?

My mother knew no limits! She was on a first name basis with Ken and Bob and if God had a first name, she wouldn't hesitate to use it. Doug was right. My mother communicated regularly with people in high places.

"Did you get enough to eat, David?"

"Yep, that chocolate pie hit the spot! Um, that's why I like to eat at the Quarrier Diner when we come to Charleston. It has fresh homemade pies."

Mother agreed, giving David a slight nudge. "Hurry or we will miss the bus."

After paying the cashier and exiting, the two speeded up and cut through the alley which came out by Sam's Pawn Shop. That is where David came to an abrupt halt. He could not pass by Sam's without checking out all the treasures in the window: watches, diamond rings, guitars, knives, etc. "Mom, the first job I get I'm going to buy you a diamond ring just like that big one over there." He pointed, placing another smudge on the already dirty window.

"I think I've heard that before." Mom started singing, "I'll buy you a diamond ring, and if that ring don't shine, I'll buy . . ." She stopped her singing abruptly, "Look, there is a set of used his and her wedding bands. Sad, isn't it?"

"Why?" questioned David.

"Oh, you are too young to understand. Come on, the bus will be here." She grabbed David by the elbow.

But just as they started past the open door, David applied his brakes again. "Wow, look at that blue pearl bass drum!"

"That thing with ECHO written across the front?" Mother asked, as she pointed into the darkened interior of the pawn shop.

"Let's take a look." David, not waiting for an answer, walked inside. Mom followed.

"Hi, Nadine. Haven't seen you for a while," greeted Sam, the owner, from the shabby chair in which he was sitting.

Mother flashed her familiar friendly smile and walked over to exchange niceties, as David looked at the drum.

133

"I sure would like to have this drum. I got those used snares but no bass. Where is the footpedal?" David turned and looked at Sam.

"There ain't no footpedal. That's why I have to sell it so cheap—ten dollars you can have it for."

"Wow, did you hear that, Mom?"

"Um, do those cymbals go with it, Sam? Those with no stand over there on the floor?" asked Mother with little enthusiasm.

Sam stood up and slid his hands in his pant pockets. "Being you're an old customer, I'll throw those in too."

"Please, Mom!"

Mother reached in her big black purse and pulled out a crumpled five dollar bill. "Allowing for bus fare, this is all I have."

Sam reached over and snatched the five out of Mother's hand. "It's a deal," said Sam. "You always did drive a hard bargain, Nadine."

"Um," was Mother's only response.

"Oh, Momma, thank you, thank you, thank you!" David plopped a kiss on her cheek. Then asked "How are we going to get that big drum and set of cymbals home? It's too bulky for the bus."

"And, we can't roll it twelve miles from Charleston to St. Albans," Mother said as the two wrinkles right above her nose deepened—her "think harder" wrinkles. "Sam, can you keep it here for a couple of days—till I figure a way to get it home?"

"Why not? Been here a year already. What's a couple more days?" Sam said as he slid the five into his pocket with a motion that caused clinking of coins.

Trying to get the drum and cymbals home before Dad returned from a hunting trip, Mother made arrangements for a Charleston cab to pick the drums up at Sam's and take them to the Greyhound Bus Station. Then the drum and cymbals were to travel via bus to St. Albans where they would be picked up at the bus depot by the St. Albans Cab Company and delivered to 825 Saunders Street.

Arrangements were made, and the drums were on their trip to St. Albans when Mother placed her call to the St. Albans Cab Company. "St. Albans Cab, Joe here." the dispatcher answered.

Mother hesitated for a minute, thrown off by the unfamiliar voice. "I need to speak to Al."

"Ain't here."

"Where is he?"

"How should I know, Lady? Just work here."

"Where is his son, Pete?"

"Lady, what's this, roll call? This here is a business phone, not for social chatter. Do you want a cab or not?"

Mother, intent on her mission, was not going to let this young upstart deter her. "An Echo drum will be arriving at 5:30 p.m. at the Greyhound Depot and needs picked up," she said.

"Does he know I'm coming?"

"It's not a he, sir."

"You mean there's a woman by the name of Echo Drum?" asked the cab dispatcher with surprise.

"It's not a woman, sir."

"Not a he or she but one of them, huh?" the voice came back.

"It's a drum and set of cymbals, sir. I want them placed in the back seat, just as any other passenger."

"By any chance am I talking to the lady I make regular runs to the liquor store for?"

"Well, I never!" retorted Mother. "This is Nadine Erwin at 825 Saunders Street, a lifetime member of the First Baptist Church, and I do not indulge, sir."

"Never'd know you didn't indulge by talking to you, Ma'am."

The clink of the telephone receiver was Mother's response to that. But everybody has a price, and for a price of a passenger's fare, the drum and cymbals were delivered. It is estimated that David's beginning drum + transportation + footpedal + stand for cymbals cost fifty-eight dollars.

UP A TREE

"Hello."

"David, this is Patty. How is everything?"

"Usual, you calling from school?"

"Yeah, I need to talk to Mom. Hurry! remember this is long distance."

"Mom is pretty busy, but I'll try to get her attention."

At that, David left me dangling.

"Is this my college girl?" came Mother's jovial voice.

"Mother, David said you are busy. What's happening?"

"I was watching Joe up in the sycamore tree."

"When I was little you told me about Zacchaeus, the tax collector, in the sycamore tree, not Joe," I teased.

"Well, two thousand years later in St. Albans, West Virginia, it is Joe, the fireman, in the sycamore tree, not Zacchaeus."

"Why is Joe perched in the tree? Is the St. Albans Fire Department having ladder drill in Bowman's sixty-foot sycamore?"

"No, there is a cat up there. They are trying to get it down."

"I am sure that cat is a more astute climber than any of the firemen. It will come down when everybody goes away. Who would be dumb enough to call the fire department to get a cat out of a tree, anyway?"

"I did, and no, the cat, which is actually a kitten, can't get down."

"How do you know?"

"David's dog chased the poor little thing up the tree. It has been up there all afternoon, meowing. I hoisted David up on my shoulders to get it, but the kitten climbed higher. Then I put a bowl of milk under the tree. Kitty tried to come down but was too scared."

"You mean you called the fire department, and they just came splitting to rescue a cat out of a tree. That's next to rescuing a bird out of a tree."

"No," answered Mother, "The smart alec I first spoke to said he had better things to do than rescue cats. He was probably busy pouring over his newest issue of *Playboy*."

"But you did not give up?"

"Right, I started to phone the Mayor, but I had talked to him about something earlier. So, I called the fire station again and asked for Cousin Joe. He got the firemen moving. Even brought a truck with a twenty-four-foot ladder."

"And all over a dog chasing a kitten up a tree," I interjected.

"A sixty-foot sycamore tree, not a mere dogwood," she quickly added. "Sometimes I feel like killing that dog."

I had to laugh. "You don't mean that little puppy that someone dropped. You stayed up nights and fed it with an eye dropper and finally my doll bottle."

"Well," answered Mother, "I envisioned its growing to the size of a Toy Poodle, not a Saint Bernard with the negative disposition of a Doberman."

"A Doberman that can strip the ticking off a mattress and the upholstery off a chair faster than a piranha can strip the flesh off a man, and with as much relish," I added.

"Well, Mother, I don't want to keep you from all the excitement. I just wanted to let you know that I have a sore throat and won't be home this weekend."

"And, I made you rice pudding too," Mother said regretfully. "Are you taking anything for your throat?"

"I'll get something. See you next weekend, bye now." I hung the phone up. Feeling feverish, I went to bed, and sleep came quickly. I was awakened by a sharp rapping on my apartment door. Looking at the clock, I was surprised that I had been asleep for over two hours. I slipped into my robe and went to the door. Peering into the dimly lit hallway, I saw

David. He was holding a big brown paper bag and shoe box with two holes in the top.

David, not waiting to be invited, came in, deposited his belongings on the sofa, and sat down.

"David, what are you doing forty miles from St. Albans? Are you running away from home? How did you get here?" I asked, wondering if I were still asleep and dreaming.

"I'm not running away from home. Mother sent me on the Greyhound to bring these." From the bag he pulled a box of tissues, a Kerr canning jar with my rice pudding, a bottle of medicine, and a box of Aspergum.

"Everything but an asaphidity bag? This looks like a commercial," was my reaction.

"Mother has added her own personal touch," said David as he took the top off the shoe box. From within came a soft "meow" and out peeked two round yellow eyes.

"I take it this was the kitten in the tree, and the firemen were successful."

"Right," said David.

"But we can't have animals in these apartments!" I protested.

A wide teasing smile broke across David's face, "Nadine's daughter will think of some way to keep the kitten," he said.

"I never claimed to be a chip off the old block, but I'll try," we laughed, anticipating my challenge. "Do you think the world's prepared for Nadine number II?"

"As ready as it was for Nadine number I," was David's response.

A

TIME

TO

PLUCK

UP

TRANSITION

While waiting for Mother to go to lunch, I glanced out my car window. The multi-colored border of crocuses along Tryall's side walk caught my eye. This first sign of spring after a long cold winter perked me up.

The crocuses, too, triggered memories of the day when I watched old Mr. Tryall through our front window. He sat on a milkstool placing bulbs in the ground, stopping frequently to catch his breath, then continuing his task.

I heard Dad come into the living room. His breath was labored as he rushed about getting ready for work. He had worked day shift since his first heart attack.

Pointing in Mr. Tryall's direction I asked, "Wonder why he's planting those flowers? He will never live to enjoy them."

Dad, sitting down and leaning over to tie his shoes, answered without hesitation, "No, but he knows others will."

My eyes then focused on the sugar maple trees next to our porch that Dad had planted and tenderly nursed until they took off on their own. *People would enjoy the maples for years after Dad is gone.*

Dad's voice broke into my thoughts, "Nadine, I'll take these sofa arm covers to the cleaners after work today. Oh, and I want to go visit Mr. Tryall this evening. I doubt he'll be with us much longer." Not waiting for an answer, Dad ran his hand over his neatly combed hair, put his hat on, slipped into his red and black checked mackinaw, picked up his lunch and walked out the door.

I fought to grab the edge of consciousness only to be sucked into the whirlpool of horror that lay in my subconscious. Struggling, I could hear my voice calling, but no help came. Pulled back into the dream, I again faced the dark figure. I sensed the suffering of this male form silhouetted in the open door, but I could not help. *I must escape*, I thought, as I forced one more scream.

"What's wrong?" came Doug's voice.

I opened my eyes, looking around the soft blue bedroom where the only shadows were patterns of sunlight filtering through lacy curtains. *I'd escaped*, I thought, but relief was replaced by anxiety and overwhelming sadness. Sobs now in my consciousness replaced the screams of my subconsciousness.

"It's a bad dream. You're Okay, now!" Hearing the reassurance of Doug's voice, my sobs began to subside.

"What was so bad?" he questioned.

Trying to make sense in my conscious mind of what transpired in my dream, I began to describe the desperate figure of my dream. "I heard a sound at our front door; there was a man."

"What did he say?"

"He never spoke. He only stood there motionless, almost engulfed by the early morning fog. He was seeking help."

"How do you know?"

I probed deeper, trying to recall details of my dream. Distracted by the effort to recall, my sobs now were replaced by salty warm tears seeking the corners of my mouth. My body flinched as the image focused. "It was like a portion of his head was missing or that I couldn't see it because he was bleeding profusely."

"Who was this person?" Doug's voice showed concern.

"I never saw his face because of the bleeding. I just knew I loved him; he needed help; and I lacked the power to do anything. It was beyond my control. I had to go for help, to escape."

"Well I'm supposed to be the only man in your life, and I'm here, see?"

The *silliness of a dream*, I tried to rationalize, but the sadness, anxiety and yes, even remorse persisted.

Doug's words broke into my thoughts. "Well it's 8:00 a.m. Time for people who work for a living to get up."

I knew he was only joking about me as a teacher, since I was on Christmas break.

"What are your plans for the day?" he asked.

"Janet and I are going to hit the after Christmas sales."

Strange how I can remember twenty-six years ago what I wore shopping: a blue, black and white tweed skirt, white blouse trimmed in lace and flat black shoes, a part of my Christmas gifts.

The challenge of finding good buys took my mind from the dream. Driving home, Janet and I discussed the money we had saved, not what we had spent. As we neared home, our conversation was interrupted by her question, "Can you come over for a cup of coffee?"

"No, I'd better go straight home today." I looked up, at that moment, and saw Doug driving toward us on Kanawha Terrace. "He should be at work; something is wrong."

Seeing Janet and me, Doug pulled onto the berm. Janet followed his lead.

"I'll go with him," I volunteered, getting out of her car.

Doug began when I got into our car. "I really hate to tell you this," he said, resting his hand on my shoulder. He paused to measure each word. "I have bad news—bad news

145

about your dad." Doug's voice broke. "Vinson died at work today."

In the gap between Doug's words and my response, the chilling anxiety that I experienced earlier in the day now had a reason for being. Since sixteen years earlier my dad had suffered a serious heart attack, my question was, "He died of a heart attack?"

"No, he died from a blow to the head. The man who came from DuPont to tell your mother said that the workman who collected the water samples your dad took from Kanawha River to check pollution levels made his first round at 7:00 a.m. and your dad was fine. When the workman made his second round, he found Vinson and an overturned ladder. The men from DuPont asked your mother's permission for an autopsy which she gave."

The autopsy report showed my father had a heart arrest, but the cause of death was brain damage. We believed that he was on the ladder opening the valves which adjusted release of waste water, when he had his heart arrest. Then he fell from the ladder, hitting the concrete. The blow to the head resulted in death. It was estimated that the time of death was somewhere between 7:00-8:00 a.m. that morning. I could never ask if death came immediately.

I know God gave me a glimpse into the future to soften the news of Dad's accident. I will always be grateful for the prior warning, for I had never known life without my father.

This remembrance still brought tears to my eyes. I didn't want to go to a restaurant with red eyes, so I was relieved when I heard the front door open and saw Mother. With a smile and a flick of her wrist, she gave me a quick wave of recognition. Carefully holding to the banister, she descended the steps one at a time.

Dad's death changed Mother. Some of her spunk was gone and, with David and me both married, she relinquished her role as nurturer. Even with all this and her declining health,

146

Mother clung to her sense of humor. Having had most of her back teeth pulled by age sixty-five she would say, "I feel like the old woman, who when asked what she had to be thankful for answered, 'That I have two teeth and that they hit together.'"

So the human drama of the Erwin family continued to unfold, minus the character of Vinson. That is, if one believes people die. I believe they continue to live within the people they have touched.

One snowy Thursday morning, I was talking to Mother on the phone when there came a rap on her door. She put me on hold, saying she had to let the garbage man in. I was left to wonder why the garbage man needed to come in, perhaps to collect an unpaid sanitation bill or to sell tickets to the garbageman's ball? No, that couldn't be right. It was the policeman's ball. Then Mother's voice came over the line, "Hello, hello, hello, are you still there?"

"Just as you left me. What was the garbageman doing in the house?"

"Picking up the garbage," was her reply. "Patty, it's cold outside."

"So?"

"Whenever it's cold, Jackson comes inside to get my garbage. Buena Isabell, his sister, and I went to the eighth grade together, you know. She didn't have any teeth, poor girl."

"You mean beautiful Isabell was toothless?"

"As toothless as a hen. At lunch, she always had to suck on her carrot stick."

"It sounds like you're almost kissing cousins to Jackson and his sister," I said a little grudgingly. I had to tug my own garbage cans from the backyard to the front curb and practically put a Christmas ribbon on the lid to get it picked up.

Then there was the mailman. Mother would leave him notes:

Dear Mr. Postman:
Could you bring me a book of
stamps as I'm out. Here is my check.
Thank you, Nadine
P.S. Set mail inside on the desk. Birds are nesting
in my mailbox.

Justin, the mailman, never failed to comply with these requests. There were certain things, however, at which he balked.

For example, when Mother's friend Ruby lost her brother, Mother immediately mailed her condolences. The next day, Justin knocked on Mother's door; when she opened it, he placed the sympathy card in her hand.

"Why are you returning Ruby's card? There is a stamp on it." She pointed to the corner of the envelope.

"Yes," Justin agreed.

"My return address is on it."

"That's right."

"And Ruby's full name, Ruby Beatrice Kiff," she pointed to each item.

Justin in turn pointed to each item as he read, "Ruby Beatrice Kiff, St. Albans. That just doesn't hack it, Nadine. The post-office has to have a complete address."

"But I don't know Ruby's address."

"Neither do I, Nadine."

"How will I ever find it?" Concern showed in her voice. "If I have to call Ruby and ask her what her address is, it will take all the surprise out of her getting the sympathy card."

"Nadine, use your phone directory."

"Why don't you, Justin?"

"Why don't you, Nadine?" He turned and went down the steps yelling over his shoulder, "I'll get the card tomorrow. Just leave it on your desk."

Mother was disappointed in Justin. "I helped his mother pick out that boy's first pair of roller skates when I was working at Leonard's Hardware. He wasn't brought up to be rude to old people. I'll tell you that."

She was recounting all of this as I looked up Ruby's address in the phone book.

Mother's sphere of influence did not stop with the garbageman nor the postman.

"Mother, I wish you would go to the League of Women Voters' meeting with me tonight. I'll be leaving the house at 6:30 and be home by 9:30."

"Why would I want to go to a League of Women Voters' meeting?"

"It affords you the opportunity to speak out on important government issues and to learn how to influence government officials in decision making."

"I don't have to go to a meeting to talk about the government. I can do that at home."

"But, Mother, to get things done you have to be a part of a group; there is power in numbers, and it will give you clout."

"Clout? Is that something I can't do without?"

"Oh, forget it, Mother. I'll talk to you tomorrow and tell you what I've learned about the effectiveness of lobbying to get things done."

"That will be fine. I'm going to watch Chief Big Ugly and Philip the Fair in the championship wrestling match tonight on television to see how physical force is used to get things done. You be careful. Snow is predicted."

Sure enough snowflakes started dropping about 4:00 that afternoon. The flakes increased in number, accumulating on my hillside to the point that traffic halted. No League meeting tonight, I thought disappointedly. I'll be staying home.

I was finishing up the supper dishes around 6:00 when I heard a loud rumbling and saw the reflection of a rotating red light flashing from the street into my livingroom. Then I heard men's voices; salt was being put on the street. The salt truck had arrived just in time. I quickly got into my warmest winter clothes, grabbed my car keys, and followed the salt truck off the hill. I'd worry about getting back up when the time came. However, to my surprise, on my return trip I met the salt truck coming off my hill. I was in luck. The hill had been treated twice in three hours.

Unable to wait until the next day to share my new found knowledge on how to influence government and get things done, I phoned Mother.

Her opening statement was, "You got up and down your hill without any trouble, didn't you?"

"Yes, but how did you know?"

"The Mayor gave me his word," she said.

"The Mayor gave you his word about what?"

"I called and told him you had an important meeting to go to and the hill had to be cleared at 6:30 and 9:30, so you could get through. He said he would get right on it."

"Mother, you mean you called the Mayor at his home?"

"Well, yes. I've known Averil Ramsey all my life. He sold your dad and me our cemetery lots."

"Mother, you should have called the Street Department, not the Mayor."

"Patty, you know the principle of power in numbers that you were talking about?"

"Yes, we discussed that issue tonight."

"Well, there is another important principle to know; it saves time to go straight to the top. You will probably discuss this source of power next week."

I had to admit my mom certainly knew where the source of power was, whether it was getting indoor pickup by the garbageman, home delivery of stamps by the mailman, or a street salted by the mayor, so her daughter could attend an "important meeting" to learn how to get things done.

We were sitting in line at the drive-in bank window. Mother was writing her check. Upon completion, she ripped out the check and handed it to me. Then she tucked her checkbook back into her purse.

"You didn't enter your withdrawal in your checkbook, Mother."

"I didn't do what?"

"You didn't write down how much you wrote your check for."

"I never do," she answered.

"You're kidding. Let me see your checkbook."

Watching her dig deeply into her purse, I saw an Easter egg make its way to the top as she dug deeper and deeper.

"Mother, what are you doing carrying a boiled Easter egg in your purse?"

"That's my lunch. I'm on a diet."

I wrinkled my nose as if I smelled something and to show my disapproval.

"You can't waste a perfectly good boiled egg. Easter was only yesterday. Now here's my checkbook."

I opened the check register. It was as clean as the day it was issued. Holding it up, I pointed to the unspoiled pages. "It's blank, Mother!"

"So, what's the big deal?"

"Well, how do you know how much you have left in the bank if you never subtract the amount of the checks you write?"

"I call Mrs. Burnside at the bank. You know, your Aunt Audrey's niece, and I ask her what I've got left. She is real nice about telling me."

The car behind me honked, and I responded by moving up to the bank window, cashing the check, and driving off the lot. Mother was smiling and waving at everybody. I felt as though I were transporting the homecoming queen.

I reopened the subject as we headed toward Charleston. "But Mother, the figure she gives you is not actually what you have to work with."

"Hush your mouth, child. You mean Audrey's niece is a liar, and here I see her going to church every Sunday?"

"No, Mrs. Burnside is not lying to you. She is telling you how much money there is in your checking account at the time you call. But you would have checks out which haven't arrived at the bank yet. If you write checks equal to the amount Mrs. Burnside says you have, you'll end up overdrawn."

Mother looked puzzled, "You would think those high falootin bankers would think of a better system than that of taking care of my money."

"Mother, it's not their responsibility to keep track of your checking account to see that you don't spend more money than you have."

"That's what they get paid for, isn't it?"

"Not exactly Mother." I emphasized each of those words.

Mother, sensing my exasperation, said, "Let's go to Rose City Cafeteria and get some chicken-dumplings and pecan pie. That will make us both feel better."

"I thought you were on a diet."

"I can hold the Easter egg over another day. Let's go."

I pondered Mother's checking situation all through lunch. Between my main course and dessert, I made the decision to go to the library. Here I checked out a projector and a filmstrip.

Seeing me put the library material in the car, Mother was all smiles. "What are we going to see a movie about?"

"How to balance your checkbook."

Her enthusiasm cooled quickly. "Sounds dry as a bone to me."

Seated in her darkened livingroom, I flashed the film onto the wall. "I can't hear anything," said Mother, "Have I gone deaf? It's bad enough to have my kidneys kick out on me."

"You haven't gone deaf; there is no sound. You're supposed to read the caption below each picture."

"I like the ones with sound." She jumped up, went to the kitchen and came back carrying a cup of coffee. "Do you want something to drink?"

"No."

Halfway into the film, I missed Mother again and heard a popping sound in the kitchen. I flipped off the projector and waited.

Mother reentered the room with a bowl of popcorn and a salt shaker. "You can't have a movie without popcorn." Sensing my disapproval, she added, "Chewing always helps me think better."

"Mother, now let's be serious."

"That's your problem, Patty; you're too serious. All work and no play makes Johnny a dull boy. In your case . . ."

"Please, Mother. Now we've played enough," I said, flipping the projector back on, "I'm trying to teach you a life skill."

She tilted her head just slightly to the right and looked at me with her knowing look and said, "I've never had a check to bounce; have you?"

I flipped the projector off, and she flipped the light on.

When we went to the bank the next week, she wrote her check, not making any entry. I didn't say a word, realizing again that Mother was more skilled in life than I would ever be. It was Mother who had Mrs. Burnside, the bank teller, as her personal accountant, not I.

THE CLEANING LADY COMETH

"Now, Patty, be sure to get a real nice boneless roast with just a ribbon of fat down the center, so it will be juicy and tender—no gristle; lemons for fresh lemonade; and some nice green beans."

"How many cans of beans, Mother?"

"Not canned beans, Patty, fresh half-runners. Oh, yes, and a ham hock, to flavor them with."

"For whom are you going to all the trouble of stringing beans and squeezing lemons? The preacher coming?"

"No, Patty, the cleaning lady."

"What cleaning lady did you get?"

"Mrs. Black's said she'd come tomorrow."

"Did you get any references on the lady? Can't be too careful, now days."

"She cleans for Mrs. Black, doesn't she?" was Mother's answer.

"In fact, it was the other way around, of sorts."

"You mean you had to give the cleaning lady references."

"Gert, that's the lady's name, said she'd have to come look at my house before she could give me an answer. That's why I'm not going to the store with you. I'm pooped from cleaning all yesterday, getting ready for Gert's inspection."

"You have to be joking," was my reaction.

"No, I tried to tell Gert, over the phone, that my house wasn't much different from Mrs. Black's, but no, she insisted on checking it out herself."

"When does this white glove inspection take place?"

"Already has. She came this morning, and I passed." Mother said with pride.

Then she saw me eyeing the cobwebs up in the corners and table legs which could take some washing and waxing. "I kept the drapes drawn and lights dim," she said in answer to my yet unasked question.

After going to the grocery store, helping string beans, and squeezing lemons, I went on my way, not returning until the day after the cleaning lady came.

As I walked through the living room into the dining room, heading for the kitchen where I heard Mother washing dishes, I observed the same cobwebs and table legs in need of cleaning plus a now broken lamp. Coming to the kitchen door, I saw Mother scrubbing the pots and pans in which Gert's meal had been prepared.

"Did Gert just come for lunch and then leave?" I questioned.

Mother gave a little jump. "You scared me. I didn't hear you come in. No, no, Gert and I had a real nice visit. Gert just went on and on how good my beans and everything were."

"Now that the house and your cooking have met with Gert's satisfaction, when is she going to get down to cleaning?"

Mother, shaking her head, answered, "Gert's not in good health. She has had it rough all her life. She was just worn out from cleaning Mrs. Black's house, having an allergy to dust and all. Good thing I dusted and cleaned before she came."

"Surely she could have taken a broom and knocked down some cobwebs and gotten down and washed the jelly off the dining room table legs," I said with some disgust.

Mom shrugged, "I asked Gert about that. Seemed shocked that I hadn't heard about her bad back. She asked if I wanted to be responsible for her going into the hospital to be put in traction again? Of course I said, no."

"Of course," I echoed.

"Let's have a cup of coffee. I sure am tired," Mom said.

"Before the coffee, I want to know what happened to break the lamp."

"Gert said she had to take a fifteen-minute break after such a delicious lunch. I think she must have dozed, and her head sort of shifted on the arm of the sofa hitting the lamp."

"Looks like the cleaning lady cometh and goeth with your food and money and leaveth cobwebs and a broken lamp," I said as I finished the dishes, and Mother poured the coffee.

"Gert and I had such a good time, and that is what's important at my age anyway. Besides, those cobwebs have been around so long, we've become old friends. Now let's not waste any more time talking about Gert."

"That's fine with me," I agreed.

"Well, just one more thing," Mother said. "Before I forget, Gert said she would like chicken and dumplings for lunch next week."

"Hello, Clem's Jot um' Down Store, Nadine speaking."

"Mother, stop your joking. This is Patty."

"Figures."

"Were you expecting me to call?"

"Nope!"

"Then what do you mean, figures?"

"Only two people call me Mother, you and your brother."

I smiled to myself at this answer.

"I'd be in real trouble if I couldn't tell the difference between you and David. And you'd be in worse trouble," she added.

"Okay, Okay," I said and laughed. "So, what are you doing?"

"Nursing."

That answer caught me off guard. "Nursing, who's sick?"

"Not that kind of nursing. I'm nursing a rabbit."

Following a few seconds of pondering, I ventured, "You're nursing a rabbit?"

"With an eye dropper and warm milk," Mother replied.

"Where did you get a rabbit?"

"Well, it's really a bunny. Wampum was stalking it when I came to the rescue."

"But that cat only has three legs," I interjected.

"Wampum has adapted," she said. "He stalks bunnies now instead of rabbits. Old age and an amputated leg have not dampened his hunting instincts."

"Speaking of instinct, Mother, you have always had an inborn feeling for the care of animals. When Wampum had his leg amputated, you knew just what to do, staying up nights and everything."

"Comes more from being raised on a farm than inborn. Mom, Mrs. Taylor, taught me."

I remained silent, hoping Mother would continue. Life was so different when she was a little girl. Going from Poca to Charleston, for example, meant traveling by horse and buggy to Nitro, stabling the rig at Bateman's and then on to Charleston by steamboat, *The Evergreen*. Mother's description of dinner—boarding-house style—aboard *The Evergreen* on the return trip sounded so romantic. How I loved hearing these stories of Mother's childhood; a time not so distant, yet in lifestyle so far removed.

"I never will forget," she reminisced, "a big ole snapping turtle tore one of our ducklings' tails off. Mom, Mrs. Taylor, took that little duckling and sewed its tail right back on, keeping the little one in the chicken coop until its bottom healed."

"Hmmm," I said to let Mother know that I was listening but not to interrupt her story.

"Well, that duckling took right up with those chickens, following the hen as if she were her very own Momma."

"Yes, there's a name for that," I replied.

Mom went on, "But Mrs. Taylor was practical. When an animal was dead, it was dead and buried. No tears wasted.

"Once a chick died, and Elizabeth, Mrs. Taylor's niece, and I had the chick a funeral. We used a kitchen matchbox for a casket, sang hymns, and preached over it. But I questioned how there could be proper mourning without a wake. So, Elizabeth and I sneaked the dead chick up to my bedroom.

"After everybody went to bed, we set the tiny casket and its contents in my window sill. As the full moon slowly positioned itself on our window, silhouetting the casket and its contents, the chick gave the appearance of growing larger and larger and larger! I convinced Elizabeth that the dead chick was indeed levitating. This vision, combined with low moaning and groaning, supplied by yours truly, and an occasional

159

'Whoo! whoo! whoo!' from the owl in the big oak tree set Elizabeth to screaming and carrying on."

Mother stopped and commenced giggling. Her mind's eye had allowed her to travel back in time, once more a little girl.

"Well, you guessed it," Mother went on; "Mrs. Taylor came in to see what all the commotion was and caught us in the middle of the wake. She snatched up the feathered corpse, admonishing us about the dreaded disease which we were sure to contract for handling the dead fowl; that was that."

"And that mischievous little girl grew up to be my mischievous mother," I said. We laughed together knowing that truth is truth.

"Here came Shirley dragging that proverbial basket of flowers into May's funeral service," Mother gossiped on, as we munched cookies and sipped coffee. "He was late and lit up as usual. Causing a lot of commotion, stepping over and on people, getting the basket in place, Shirley settled in by yours truly," Mother said pointing to herself.

"I kept my eyes focused on the preacher, so Shirley wouldn't try to pull me into one of his long involved discourses. They delivered him home drunk in a wheelbarrow the other night, you know," Mother interjected as just a side note.

"Anyway, the preacher, trying to ignore all the ruckus continued, 'The Lord giveth and the Lord taketh away.' "

" 'THAT'S AS SQUARE A DEAL AS I EVER HEARD,' Shirley said, shaking his head sadly. Everybody, including the preacher, turned and stared at him. He of course took no notice, remaining solemn faced."

Mother broke off her account of May's funeral and turned her attention to me. "Patty, do you have to be somewhere at a certain time?"

Setting my cup of coffee on the dining room table where we sat, I shook my head.

"Then why are you staring at the clock?"

"I was just wondering."

"Wondering what?"

"I was just wondering, with the many conventional means such as nails, screws, and toggle bolts, why you chose to hang the electric clock on a prong of a fork stuck in the wall?"

"That?" she questioned, motioning toward the clock.

"Right," I nodded.

"Clever, don't you think?" She smiled and explained, "I can adjust the level of the clock by just moving it from one prong to the other."

"I admit, most people wouldn't think of that but . . . . ."

"Well, I tried those little hooks which you paste on the wall. That's conventional, isn't it?" Mother looked for my reaction.

"Yes," I agreed.

"They're supposed to hold up to five pounds, but the hooks kept coming unglued. The clock fell down; I don't know how many times," she said with a shrug.

The dried yellow glue marks encircling the small white plastic clock testified to the truth of Mother's account.

"Your dad never wanted nails driven into the plaster, you know. Besides, the hole was already there. That's where the wires came out for the doorbell chimes—the chimes that got lost. Remember?" She looked at me again for confirmation. "Getting frustrated with the stickers, I just rammed the fork into the hole. Works fine, don't you think?"

Groping for the right answer, I paused too long, and Mother went on. "Those stickers are just one example of the frustrations old people have to endure. Here's another," she said, holding up exhibit two.

I stared at the jagged glass edge which was all that remained of the neck of the lidless aspirin bottle.

"They just keep improving things until they're totally useless. I think it is a conspiracy against us old people."

"You don't really mean that, Mother?"

"I do! Here I am seeking some relief from the pain in my stiff, crippled, arthritic hands, so I screw and screw the lid of this aspirin bottle, to no avail. Finally, with a magnifying glass—because my bifocals are all fogged up—I see in teeny tiny letters directions on how I should align a little bitty arrow up to an itty bitty dot on the bottle. The top is supposed to flip right off."

"And?"

"Murphy's law kicked in. After tearing my fingernails to the quick trying to pry the lid off, I stomped to the basement, got the screw driver, and tried to pry the lid open."

"I take it that didn't work?"

"Right on! By this time, I'm writhing in pain with relief in the form of little white pills clearly visible through this glass bottle. So I just took the screw driver handle and smashed the cap off the bottle."

"Those are child-proof bottles, Mother."

"Are you saying I'm a child?"

"No, Mother, I was just explaining why medicine bottles are designed that way." But no stopping her now, Mom was on a roll.

She fumed, "Then there's the clothes dryer."

Exhibit three, I thought. Why had I ever asked the question that brought all of this on, or had I?

Mother leaned across the table to assure eye contact and undivided attention. "I haven't had a pair of matching socks since I got that clothes dryer."

"I thought only Billy goats and silverfish ate clothes," I joked.

"Wrong! Add clothes dryers to that list. But, I'm going to outsmart that machine," she said confidently. "I'm saving all the odd socks, waiting for that DAY!"

She now had a far away gleam in her eyes. Drawn into the spell, I whispered, "What day?"

"The day of the great abortion."

"The day of what?"

"When the dryer aborts those long lost socks."

I could picture this great eruption of odd socks spewing forth from the belly of the machine.

"Then there's that plastic commode seat."

"Mom! What on earth are you talking about now?"

"I was just giving another example of how they keep improving things until they become totally useless, or in this case, down right dangerous."

"How could a commode seat be dangerous?"

"A bolt that held the wooden seat to the commode tank came out and got lost. So, if you didn't balance yourself just right when you sat down, the seat did a quick whirl and propelled you into the floor, before you knew what was up."

"Does sound dangerous," I agreed.

"I haven't gotten to the dangerous part yet. When your dad tried to replace the seat, they said, 'No more wooden seats, just modern plastic ones.' In no time, a crack came in the seat that was only noticeable when you sat on it which Vinson was doing one morning when the telephone rang. He jumped up to answer the phone and was almost transformed from a bass to a soprano. That thing almost stripped him of his manhood."

"I think you'd better close your case with exhibit number four."

"But, there is more," she insisted.

"I don't doubt that, but you've made your point."

Mother, shaking her head, said, "I guess Shirley knows."

"About the adjustable clock hook, the old people-proof medicine bottles, the day of the great abortion, or the commode seat that assumes the personality of a snapping turtle?"

"No, that the Lord giveth and the Lord taketh away is the only square deal," she answered.

Hoping to bring this discussion about man's inhumanity to old people to a close, I agreed with Mother, "Best deal in town."

TEETH

"Mother, I refuse to take you to dinner if you don't wear your teeth." Mother gave me a cutting look and went back into the house to get her false teeth.

"You certainly look pretty tonight, Mother," I said, after placing our dinner order.

"Don't feel very pretty; these teeth never have fit." With her tongue, she moved her lower dentures out of her mouth and quickly retrieved them the same way. Then she flipped them up and down making a clicking sound.

"I get the point, Momma." I looked around to see if anyone noticed. A boy about two was laughing and pointing at Mother.

Recognizing that she had an audience, Mother stuck her teeth out again. The little boy let out a loud howl. His mother looked across the restaurant to see why he was laughing. Mother quickly retrieved her teeth, took on her air of sophistication and smiled at the boy's mother.

"Mother," I said in a low scolding tone. I looked down to straighten my napkin and heard one more click.

Upon finishing our meal, I told Mother that I would pay the bill while she went to the restroom. "When you finish, I'll be in the car, Okay?" Mother nodded her head in agreement.

I sat in the car patiently waiting. Mother did not appear.

Finally, I went back inside and checked out the dining room and restroom—no Mother. Checking to see if there was another exit, I heard a commotion in the kitchen.

As a waitress flung the kitchen door open, I caught a glimpse of Mother. Her face was puckered up like a dried apple doll's. She paced back and forth through garbage strewn

165

on the floor, ringing her hands in distress, saying, "What will I do? Whatever will I do?"

The busboy was bent over the garbage can frantically looking for something.

I stepped inside. "What are you doing, Mother?" She ignored my question. "Gotta go," she whispered to the busboy. "My daughter is here to get me." With a swift slight of hand, she palmed him a half dollar.

Almost slipping on a wet lettuce leaf as I backed out the kitchen door, I tried to regain my composure as I hustled Mother through the dining room and out the door.

We were almost to our car when I heard someone chasing us. Mother whirled about, clutching her pocketbook in one hand and raising her umbrella in a defensive stance. "Go for the groin," she directed me.

When I turned, the footsteps speeded up and I heard, "Lady wait!"

"Mother, don't attack! It's the busboy."

Upon reaching us, he handed Mother a wadded up white napkin, "I thought I never would catch you," he panted.

Mother dropped her defensive stance and cried, "Bless you, bless you!" Again there was the swift slight of hand motion, and I heard coins clink as a wide smile crossed the young man's face. Carefully she then unfolded the napkin, exposing her pearly whites. I looked at her for an explanation.

"I wrapped my teeth up in this napkin to put them in my purse, but I forgot and left them on my plate. They got dumped."

She waved good-bye to the busboy. Turning to me, she said, "See, there are lots of good people left in the world. We'll have to come back here to eat again, won't we?"

"Never," I said.

"What's wrong?" inquired Mother. "Didn't you like the food?"

PLAYMATES

Through the front window, Mother watched my son, Mark. He loved the swing in the maple tree. Pumping his chubby legs in rhythmic motions, Mark was lifted higher and higher into the air. By swinging just so high, he could watch the train wind its way along Kanawha River. It was cozy and safe here where the thick green leaves sheltered this part of the earth from the hot sun. He quit pumping, and the swing went slower and slower. Mother saw that his attention was drawn to the dancing lacy pattern beneath his feet made by the few rays of sunlight that pushed through the leaves.

She had been baby sitting for four-year-old Mark a few days a week for about a year, so I could write my dissertation. Doug had finished his doctorate just before Mark's birth.

Mother's friends asked what Doug did for a living, and after several frustrating attempts of trying to recall Director of Research, Planning and something and something, she answered, "All I know is he has a secretary and works in an office in Charleston." She said to me once, "Why couldn't he be a plumber? I could have remembered that."

Hearing a deep rumble of thunder and sensing a change in the air, she stepped onto the porch. "Mark, come sit on the porch with Gran. Hear that bird? He's saying, 'Rain, rain, rain.' "

"Don't want to," Mark answered.

"Gran is going to fix you a baseball sandwich with grilled cheese and bologna."

Gran was the only one who made baseball sandwiches. She made the sandwich and cut it with a biscuit cutter into the shape of a ball. With this incentive, Mark half ran and half hopped to sit on the porch steps with Gran.

"Look, Mark, how the clouds are growing darker and are moving about. What does that one over there look like?"

167

"A dragon!" he answered after a few seconds of studying the shape.

"You're right, Mark. See the dull gray smoke curling out of its nostrils? And look at the tree. See how its leaves curve skyward for a cool drink of rain?" She cupped her small hands imitating the leaves.

Mark tilted his head sideways and watched this phenomenon. As the leaves lifted upward, the tree took on a silvery color. Then its branches began to sway, and the adjacent maple answered with the same movement. "They talk to each other," he said pointing at the trees.

"I swan, I believe they are." The swaying ceased. "Hush before the storm," Gran whispered.

Following this brief intermission came the soft rustling sound of the wind passing through the leaves, another rumble of thunder and a splash of one single rain drop. At this, Mark squirmed off Gran's lap and demanded, "I want baseball sandwich." Hand in hand the two walked inside the house that had sheltered her from storms for over thirty-five years.

Once inside, Mark and Gran stepped into the world of make believe. Both were equally engrossed in the antics of Bert, Ernie, and Cookie Monster which were projected on the TV screen in bright red, orange, yellow, blue and green. Cookie Monster actually materialized in the living room by way of a hand puppet Gran kept stashed under the sofa.

When Mark slowed down on his intake of the baseball sandwich, Monster jumped into Mark's lap and yelled, "I'm going to eat Mark's food."

Mark, leaning back giggling, crammed the last bite into his mouth and answered, "No, no, no, all gone."

During a commercial, which Mark watched as intently as *Sesame Street*, Gran drifted into her own thoughts, and sometimes whispered to herself, "I always wanted four children and that's what I have—Patty, Doug, David, and Linda.

It's a small world. David married Gladys Ellis' granddaughter, and Gladys was my childhood friend."

Gran's attention then turned to her grandchildren. She looked at Mark and commented on how different he and David's little girl, Rochelle, were in coloring. Mark had green eyes and blonde hair like Doug and me. Rochelle had brown eyes and was a brunette like David and Linda. Vinson would have enjoyed this expanded family which always came together to celebrate holidays and birthdays. Gran regretted not having more time with Rochelle, who lived sixty miles away in Beckley. Her thoughts and whispering were broken into.

"I'm still hungry, Gran."

"Here, Gran has you a box of animal cookies. You better gobble them up or Cookie Monster will."

Mark proceeded to line the cookies up across the coffee table to make a parade as Gran had shown him. But, instead of giraffes, tigers, and apes there were nurses, policemen and postmen.

Gran, with a cursory glance, said, "What will they think of next. Must be trying to teach kids to be cannibals."

After emptying the box, Mark bit down on the policemen's head. "Yuck!" he said, sticking his tongue out exposing the half-chewed head. "Taste bad."

Gran quickly grabbed the box, read the label, and burst out laughing. "No wonder. Spit it out, Mark. This says, People Cookies for Animals. I picked up the wrong thing. I swan, when you get old everything goes—your plumbing, then your blinkers." Gran pointed to her eyes.

"Feed them to Nicky."

The little white poodle, who waited patiently as all this eating went on, responded to his name.

Gran continued talking and shaking her head at the negatives of getting old. "The other day I picked up the Lysol can instead of hair spray and sprayed my hair. It is a wonder my hair didn't fall out or turn green."

Giving a quick glance at the clock, she said, "It's almost time for your mom. Don't forget the daisies you picked for her. Tomorrow is Saturday. We'll watch wrestling."

Gran's words fell upon deaf ears. Not deaf due to old age but by choice. Mark was too busy listening and laughing at Nicky's barks as he teased him with cookies. Mark always had a good time at Gran's, his playmate's, house. At a later date he would respond to these memories by saying, "Gran was spunky."

"For this beginning art class you will need the following supplies. Art's Art Supplies will handle all of the material needed as cheaply as you can find them anyplace, and Art's is here in town." The art instructor droned on and on.

"I thought we were here to learn to draw, not to hear a commercial for Art's Art Supply," Mother said in a raised voice.

I felt warmth rush to my face. "Sh-h-h."

"Don't shush me," Mom answered. "Art probably gives this instructor a kick back"

The man seated beside us looked over and gave me a knowing smile. *He must have a Mother too*, I thought. I looked down at my writing, so as not to make eye contact with anyone else.

The instructor continued. Either he hadn't heard, didn't care, couldn't deny the statement, or he also had a Mom. "Next week you'll need the following: sheets of paper for pastels and a fixative. Hair spray will work nicely as a fixative. Oh, yes, you'll need kneaded erasers."

He paused and then asked, "Are there any questions? Your class assignment is on the board."

Everyone was still busily finishing out the list. Hearing no questions, he said, "See you next week." Without further ado, he whirled on his heels and vanished out the door.

Walking down the corridor after class, I could see Mother's head turning to the right and then the left in a sympathetic gesture. "That poor man," she said.

"What poor man?" I asked, not seeing anyone around but us.

"The instructor."

"What's poor about him?"

"He has a speech impediment. Didn't you hear him stuttering?"

"No."

"Didn't you hear him when he said we needed needed erasers. He was so embarrassed he practically ran out the door."

"Mother, he said we needed a *kneaded* eraser. That's an art eraser. He wasn't stuttering."

"Oh," she said, "I'm glad. Bless his heart."

At first she had thought he was getting a kick back from Art's, but now he had won her over because she thought he had a handicap. That's my Mom, I thought, shaking my head and smiling as I helped her down the darkened steps into the night.

I didn't see much of Mom the following week. Whenever she got a free moment she would slip into her bedroom to do the assignment, a portrait and a tree. She was very secretive, never allowing anyone to see her art work.

I copied my assignment right out of our book about one hour before class was to begin. I was putting on the finishing touches when I heard Mother's bedroom door open and shut. There she stood, purse in hand, ready to go.

"Don't forget your assignment, Mother."

"I'm not."

"Where is it?"

"In my purse."

So when the instructor said to display our art efforts, Mother opened her big black purse and pulled out a set of pillow cases.

I heard myself draw a deep loud breath, "Mother," I managed to whisper, "you drew your pictures on your pillow cases. Why?"

"Inspiration just hit me one night; I started drawing and couldn't stop myself. Don't you like them?" she asked, rubbing over each one with her hand to remove the wrinkles.

"They're certainly original!" was my response.

The instructor was headed in our direction. "There seems to be a great deal of excitement back here with Mrs. Erwin and her daughter. Let's see what they've done."

All eyes were upon us. I remembered my family-living teacher, Mrs. Treanor, saying, "There will be times when you would just like to die. But, that doesn't mean you'll be able to." This was one of those times.

The instructor stopped short, as his eyes scanned Mother's work.

"Are those pillow cases, Mrs. Erwin?"

"What else?" she answered.

"What else indeed," he said, shaking his head. "As original as any work I've ever had a student do."

I didn't dare look up.

Deep lines formed between his eyes, as he stepped closer to scrutinize the portrait. "How did you gain that effect on the eyebrows, Mrs. Erwin?"

"I used my eyebrow pencil."

"Well, of course. I can see that now, and the hair is done in eyebrow pencil also." He turned his head this way and that to gain different perspectives.

"The skin is so white," he continued.

"That's flour, and the cheeks are done with my blush."

"Oh!" he said, "And for the lips, no doubt, you used lipstick, right!" He looked at Mother for affirmation.

"Right!" She knew they were on the same wavelength.

"Now your tree, I see you have done it on the other pillow case."

Mother, anticipating his question, supplied the answers to save him the trouble of asking. "Here, I've used crayon, chalk, eyebrow pencil, and flour. I used the flour for the snow. Then I sprayed both pictures with hair spray, as you suggested."

I was relieved; she had at least done something he had suggested.

"Mrs. Erwin, what is the irregular shaped outline around the pine tree?" He traced it with his fingers.

"A knot hole."

"A knot hole?" he questioned.

"Yes, I did this picture from one of my childhood memories. I'm seeing the tree through a knot hole."

"Under what circumstances, as a child, did you view a pine tree through a knot hole, Mrs. Erwin?"

"Whenever I went to the outdoor john!" She stopped and fixed her gaze on him. "I don't guess you know what an outdoor john is?"

"I take it you are referring to a toilet."

"That's right, Mr. Instructor. Well, if I would sit just right on the seat, I could look out a knot hole in the john door and see the prettiest little pine tree up on this hill. I can almost smell it now."

"Mrs. Erwin, I assume you are making reference to the pine tree."

"What else?" she asked, giving the instructor a blank stare.

"It's all so poetic," said the instructor.

I looked at him, then Mother, and then at my poor imitation of the picture of the tree copied out of my art book. As I looked across the room at the other students' work, I saw the same tree repeated over and over. Only Mother's was different.

Could I be hearing the instructor's words correctly as he walked back to the front of the room? "How refreshing, a spark of artistic genius is among us."

Mother, with chin tilted just slightly upward, seemed aglow with pride.

A

TIME

TO

DIE

THE PASSING

As I washed the supper dishes, I looked out upon the bare soft-gray trees with their branches reaching toward heaven. Mother sat behind me at the kitchen table flicking crumbs which I had not yet cleaned away. This was her second day home, following a three-and-a-half-week stay in the hospital due to gall bladder surgery, congestive heart failure and pneumonia.

With a loss of forty pounds during the past year, Mother had lost her rosy complexion which was now a subtle-gray, and her once rounded form was fragile and angular. She had said very little since coming home. When I heard her weak voice forming words, I stopped and listened closely. "You remember Trix?" she asked, as she continued maneuvering crumbs toward the center of the table.

"Trix?" I repeated thoughtfully.

"Trix, the stray dog that came to my house last year; the one you said I couldn't keep."

"Yes," I explained. "You see, with you sick, Mother, it would have been hard for me to go down to your house and care for him, especially with your cats, Miss Kitty and Abigail. Wouldn't it?" I hoped she would come to see my reasoning.

"Well," said Mother, gathering the crumbs into a small mound before her, "He only had one nut."

"What?" I asked, having expected some profound statement. "He only had one what?"

"One nut!" she answered, a little louder. Recognizing my lack of comprehension, she added, "I mean, Patty, he could never father puppies."

I moved closer to the table and took Mother's hand in mine. Looking into her green eyes flecked with gold, I was assured that in spite of her suffering, her comical slant on life and sense of caring lived on.

Mother's sleep that night was restless. I slept beside her bed with her tiny hand in mine. The next morning she refused breakfast and began dozing off again. Holding her hand I managed to choke out, "You are the best Mother in all the world." Her nod was positive. She then entered into a four-day coma followed by the deepest sleep of all.

Nadine Ruth Miller Erwin died without regaining consciousness January 29, 1983, while my husband, her dear friend, read to her from the Book of Ruth her favorite Bible story:

"Where you go, I will go.
Where you stay, I will stay.
Your people shall by my people,
and your God my God."

Linda and I stood silently as David unlocked Mother's front door. We had come to select a few personal items to take to the funeral home. Hearing a gentle flutter, I looked at the red-and-black wooden-rooster porch hanging that Uncle Carl had made for Mother. A scrap of paper bearing Mother's handwriting was tucked in the rooster's beak, it read:

"I'VE GOT A LOT TO CROW ABOUT!"

"A Godly man's prayers availeth much, huh, and you claim your ole man is a man of prayer. I'll bet he don't pray when there's nobody around to see him," said the man clad in khaki work clothes.

Vinson Erwin finished pouring the coffee from his thermos and waited until the steam evaporated into the air before he answered, "Yep, he does."

"How do you know?" retorted the fellow. "You see through walls?"

Vinson took a gulp of the hot coffee and slowly swallowed. "Nope, but I can see through a window pane all right."

Biting into his meatloaf sandwich, the man waited.

Vinson put his coffee down and hitched up his trousers. It would be fifteen minutes before the lunch whistle sounded, so he could leisurely linger over his explanation. "You see, I decided to drive down to spend the night with Pop. He was seventy-eight then. I knew he got awful lonesome being on the homeplace with Mom dead and all the kids gone. Living on an unpaved road up Cow Creek with the nearest neighbors four miles away, he might go several days without seeing a soul, except on Sunday when there were church services at the Adda Baptist. The church was built on a piece of land that was once part of our farm."

"Your ole man got a pretty penny for that tract of land from the good church folk, I reckon," the workman came back, wiping his mouth on the back of his hand.

"Now that's just what you know. My mom's father gave the land to build the church on."

The man rolled his eyes as if to say, "Gee, get on with this fairy tale."

"Anyway, I got a late start, and it got dark on me," Vinson continued. "I knew Pop went to bed with the chickens.

So as not to wake him, I turned my car lights and motor off, coasting into the barnyard. I'd just go in and go to bed without waking him. Poppy never locked his doors."

The man nodded as he listened.

"Well, I walked real quiet like and tip-toed onto the porch where I could see into Pop's bedroom. By the light given off by a few live coals I saw Poppy on his knees, and I heard him call my name. I listened close. He was praying for me, my family, and even my unborn grandchildren."

"Your ole man must really have been a religious fanatic praying with nobody looking and for somebody not even born yet. That's the silliest thing I ever heard of."

A knowing smile crossed Vinson's face, and he just shook his head.

Thirty years after hearing Vinson recount this conversation, I sat watching a pool of colors form on the church pew as the sunlight filtered through the stained glass window. My eyes shifted quickly in the direction of the sudden spirited cries of a baby cradled by David.

The robed minister's voice came to my ears, "By what name shall your child, whom you have brought for dedication, be called?"

David's firm clear answer could be heard above the staccato cry of the two-month-old infant, "David Patrick Erwin."

Neither the child being dedicated to God, nor his father, who held him, ever knew the old man who prayed in the empty house on Cow Creek Road. Nor would the baby know his grandfather who watched the kneeling solitary figure by the light of the ebbing embers. Vinson had been dead for over a decade. But infant Patrick would reap the benefits of the old man's prayers as would his children and their children's children.

J. V. Erwin
The old man who prayed
1953

TO

EVERYTHING

THERE IS A

SEASON

NEITHER TIME NOR PEOPLE STAND STILL

Standing in the doorway, I surveyed the empty rooms. Silent mental images of past birthdays, Mother's Days, Christmases and Easter celebrations competed for my attention; good times never to be relived. Neither time nor people stand still, I thought, as tears washed over my face.

"Wonder if Linda and I will ever have a home as nice as this again?" My brother David's voice, though amplified by the empty rooms, did not startle me, for it belonged here.

This was the second home David and I had said good-bye to in the past two years, first to the home of Nadine and Vinson and now to this one. Our eyes briefly met, and our thoughts interlocked; though reluctant, we knew we were being pulled into another phase of life.

David, clearing his throat, inventoried the house for the last time, quickly turned, and went outside where Rochelle, Doug, and Mark waited. Linda, just a few minutes earlier, accompanied by eleven-month-old David Patrick, drove her heavily laden station wagon out the driveway en route to our common destination, Greenville, South Carolina. Here David was to begin a new job.

I helped Rochelle crawl between David and her three cabbage patch dolls into the huge white and orange moving van. Mark and I then got into our car. When Doug, bringing up the rear, driving David's car, signaled, "Everything go," the engines started. We slowly began our migration south.

Unable to see in my rear-view mirror through the jungle of green house plants packed in the back of the car, I carefully adjusted the side-view mirror. As I did this, I caught a glimpse of Rochelle's three little girlfriends waving good-bye. The oldest stopped only long enough to self-consciously flip away a tear. There too, framed in the mirror, was the white birch tree planted by David several years ago.

With my eyes now focused on the bold words, "ADVENTURE IN MOVING" printed on the back of the moving van, our modern wagon train wound between mountains, through foothills, and onto the flatland. Here, on the ribbon of highway, we became engulfed by a tide of trucks, cars, vans and campers. Some were going north, some going south, others veering east and west, moving, moving, moving. The thump, thump, thump of tires crossing the seams in the highway sounded like the beating of many pulses.

An eighteen-wheeler moving van, smelling of hot rubber from overheated brakes, thundered past, flinging itself between David's van and my now dwarfed station wagon. Checking my side mirror, I was comforted by the sight of the familiar white car. This compact was crammed with household items which had spilled from David's van into my station wagon and into this rear car, sandwiching Doug between the wicker clothes hamper and the driver's door. I looked ahead to see the North American van turn onto the interstate going west and David's left turn signal announcing our lunch stop.

In this unfamiliar place, rubbing elbows with strangers, I needed only to check the menu and take a deep whiff to recognize familiar fast foods. David, Rochelle, Mark, and Doug scattered to find an outside table situated near the playground. Waiting in line for our order, I watched other hungry travelers seated in orange plastic chairs beneath leafy plants gulp down burgers and fries. I noted how seldom their eyes met and how little they spoke. We too ate in silence except for the sound of our chomping ice. We savored the cool liquid in our dry mouths.

I felt Rochelle's legs impatiently swinging back and forth beneath the table. "I'm finished. Can I play now?"

"Fries gone. And where's your hamburger?" I asked.

"Dropped on the ground," she pointed. "Now I can't eat it." Hearing no denial, she dashed off toward the swings.

Finishing our meal, we listened to the laughter and chatter shared by Rochelle and new-found friends.

"Time to go, Rochelle," I called as we quickly cleared the table.

"Do I have to? We're having fun."

As I took her hand and left the play area, I caught the eye of the mother of the two little girls still swinging. She gave me an understanding nod, and we smiled as I passed.

Our stomachs full, we quickly reassembled our caravan and started again toward Greenville. I was thankful for Mark's company—both to pass time and ward off sleep.

"Look at that old, dilapidated house," said Mark. "Do you think anyone ever lived there?"

The sun penetrated my windshield and I squinted to see the abandoned house. Its slumping gray frame and missing window panes reminded me of the gaping appearance of a toothless old woman. "Certainly someone lived there once. I even bet there was a swing right there on the porch," I answered.

Eyeing a gnarled apple tree in the yard, Mark added, "And, I bet the person who swang in the swing planted that apple tree and then moved on to Greenville just like Uncle David is doing."

"Probably," I agreed.

"Look, Mom, there goes another U-haul just like David's. It's going in the direction we just came from. How far are we from David and Linda's new home?"

"Not far, Mark." We were soon greeted by one new sub-division after another, tall glass buildings glittering in the sun, shopping malls and more shopping malls, and row after row of townhouses. Construction was everywhere making room for the modern pioneers.

Another five miles and a half dozen turns brought us to our destination, a brick-faced townhouse. Here we helped David and Linda unload. In the dining room we placed

Mother's maple table, chairs and china hutch. In the hutch, Linda carefully placed her china, an heirloom from her mother. The picture of the old man praying once again found a place over the maple table, and the conch shell used by Grandma Erwin on Cow Creek to call the field-hands to dinner served as a bookend.

Following a day of unpacking and a night's rest to heal tired backs, sore muscles and skinned knuckles, Doug, Mark and I were back in the car for our return trip. No one saw my tears. I did not want the children to sense sadness in our saying good-bye. We must be brave!

As we pulled from the curb, I heard a neighbor greeting Linda. "Where you all from?"

"West Virginia," answered Linda.

"Well, we just moved here from Spartansburg."

"You didn't have far to come."

"No matter, it's always hard to move. But after awhile, it will be like home again."

When I heard their words, something I once read came to mind, "Home is not a place but a spirit." Hopefully, a sweet spirit, I thought. But today, I knew that saying good-bye to someone seeking a new home left within me a sad spirit.

When someone I cared for left unexpectedly, I always thought how well I might have said good-bye, if only given the opportunity. Yet, how poorly I said good-bye to my brother. I simply hugged him and wished him luck, this now grown man with whom I had shared life and death. How stupid of me! I wanted to say to him, I was glad that I gave him the name David, meaning beloved; Mom and Dad would be proud of him, so sensitive, caring and responsible. I hoped, as a parent, that I could instill these fine qualities in my own son Mark, but I only said, "Good luck!"

I felt that we should act as if saying farewell is normal for the sake of the children. In their generation, unlike our parents and grandparents, who lived and died on the same plot of land, this constant churning of people would be accelerated. Neither time nor people stand still. This very moment is fleeting. As it moves, I am looking at a double framed picture with Vinson in one side and Mark in the other, realizing that the story of Nadine and Vinson has not ended. They live on, so you'd better watch out!

"To Everything There Is A Season"